MOOD JOURNAL

MONTHLY MOODS TRACKER

CHOOSE A COLOR FOR EACH OR ONLY
CERTAIN MOOD OR EMOTION.

COLOR IN EACH BOX WITH THE
COLOR OF YOUR MAIN MOOD THAT DAY.

THIS CAN HELP IDENTIFY PATTERNS.

☐ **OPTIMISTIC**
☐ **HAPPY**
☐ **EXCITED**
☐ **AVERAGE**
☐ **GRATEFUL**
☐ **SAD**
☐ **FRUSTRATED**
☐ **IRRITABLE**
☐ **RELAXED**
☐ **DEPRESSED**
☐ **CONFUSED**
☐ **MELANCHOLIC**
☐ **EMOTIONAL**
☐ **APATHETIC**
☐ **SICK**
☐ **BORED**
☐ **PANIC ATTACK**
☐ **ANXIOUS**
☐ **STRESSED**
☐ _____

NOTES:
....
....
....
....

	J	F	M	A	M	J	J	A	S	O	N	D
1												
2												
3												
4												
5												
6												
7												
9												
10												
11												
12												
13												
14												
15												
16												
17												
18												
19												
20												
21												
22												
23												
24												
25												
26												
27												
28												
29												
30												
31												

DATE: _____

Daily Mood Tracker

TODAY I FEEL

☐ grateful   ☐ motivated   ☐ satisfied   ☐ lonely   ☐ sad   ☐ tired
☐ happy   ☐ productive   ☐ calm   ☐ depressed   ☐ angry   ☐ _____
☐ proud   ☐ relaxed   ☐ powerful   ☐ anxious   ☐ annoyed ☐ _____

WHY DO I FEEL THIS WAY?

_____

_____

THREE GOALS FOR TODAY

1 _____

2 _____

3 _____

MOOD AM

😄 🙂 😐 🙁 😟 😕 😣

ENERGY LEVEL AM

1 2 3 4 5 6 7 8 9 10

STRESS LEVEL AM

1 2 3 4 5 6 7 8 9 10

MOOD PM

😄 🙂 😐 🙁 😟 😕 😣

ENERGY LEVEL PM

1 2 3 4 5 6 7 8 9 10

STRESS LEVEL PM

1 2 3 4 5 6 7 8 9 10

TODAY I HAD

	little	enough
water	☐	☐
fruits	☐	☐
vegetables	☐	☐
sleep	☐	☐
fresh air	☐	☐
free time	☐	☐
	☐	☐

👍 POSITIVE EXPERIENCES TODAY

○ success at work   ○ sports activity
○ meeting with friends ○ good weather
○ time for family   ○ time in nature
○ excursion   ○ delicious food
○ _____   ○ _____

💬 NEGATIVE EXPERIENCES TODAY

○ failure at work   ○ loneliness
○ dispute   ○ bad weather
○ criticism   ○ bad food
○ exclusion   ○ fears
○ _____   ○ _____

WHAT CAN I DO TO MAKE MY NEXT DAY BETTER?

_____

_____

THOUGHTS & REFLECTIONS

_____

_____

_____

_____

DATE: _____   DAY: M T W T F S S

Daily *Mood* Tracker

TODAY I FEEL

☐ grateful   ☐ motivated   ☐ satisfied   ☐ lonely   ☐ sad   ☐ tired
☐ happy   ☐ productive   ☐ calm   ☐ depressed   ☐ angry   ☐ _____
☐ proud   ☐ relaxed   ☐ powerful   ☐ anxious   ☐ annoyed   ☐ _____

WHY DO I FEEL THIS WAY?

_____
_____

THREE GOALS FOR TODAY

1 _____

2 _____

3 _____

MOOD AM

☺ ☺ ☺ ☹ ☹ ☹ ☹

ENERGY LEVEL AM

1 2 3 4 5 6 7 8 9 10

STRESS LEVEL AM

1 2 3 4 5 6 7 8 9 10

MOOD PM

☺ ☺ ☺ ☹ ☹ ☹ ☹

ENERGY LEVEL PM

1 2 3 4 5 6 7 8 9 10

STRESS LEVEL PM

1 2 3 4 5 6 7 8 9 10

TODAY I HAD

	little	enough
water	☐	☐
fruits	☐	☐
vegetables	☐	☐
sleep	☐	☐
fresh air	☐	☐
free time	☐	☐
	☐	☐

👍 POSITIVE EXPERIENCES TODAY

○ success at work   ○ sports activity
○ meeting with friends   ○ good weather
○ time for family   ○ time in nature
○ excursion   ○ delicious food
○ _____   ○ _____

👎 NEGATIVE EXPERIENCES TODAY

○ failure at work   ○ loneliness
○ dispute   ○ bad weather
○ criticism   ○ bad food
○ exclusion   ○ fears
○ _____   ○ _____

WHAT CAN I DO TO MAKE MY NEXT DAY BETTER?

_____
_____

THOUGHTS & REFLECTIONS

_____
_____
_____
_____

Daily Mood Tracker

TODAY I FEEL

- ☐ grateful
- ☐ happy
- ☐ proud
- ☐ motivated
- ☐ productive
- ☐ relaxed
- ☐ satisfied
- ☐ calm
- ☐ powerful
- ☐ lonely
- ☐ depressed
- ☐ anxious
- ☐ sad
- ☐ angry
- ☐ annoyed
- ☐ tired
- ☐ _____
- ☐ _____

WHY DO I FEEL THIS WAY?

_____

_____

THREE GOALS FOR TODAY

❶ _____

❷ _____

❸ _____

MOOD AM

☺ ☺ ☺ ☹ ☹ ☹ ☹

ENERGY LEVEL AM

1 2 3 4 5 6 7 8 9 10

STRESS LEVEL AM

1 2 3 4 5 6 7 8 9 10

MOOD PM

☺ ☺ ☺ ☹ ☹ ☹ ☹

ENERGY LEVEL PM

1 2 3 4 5 6 7 8 9 10

STRESS LEVEL PM

1 2 3 4 5 6 7 8 9 10

TODAY I HAD

	little	enough
water	☐	☐
fruits	☐	☐
vegetables	☐	☐
sleep	☐	☐
fresh air	☐	☐
free time	☐	☐
	☐	☐

👍 POSITIVE EXPERIENCES TODAY

- ○ success at work
- ○ meeting with friends
- ○ time for family
- ○ excursion
- ○ _____
- ○ sports activity
- ○ good weather
- ○ time in nature
- ○ delicious food
- ○ _____

👎 NEGATIVE EXPERIENCES TODAY

- ○ failure at work
- ○ dispute
- ○ criticism
- ○ exclusion
- ○ _____
- ○ loneliness
- ○ bad weather
- ○ bad food
- ○ fears
- ○ _____

WHAT CAN I DO TO MAKE MY NEXT DAY BETTER?

_____

_____

THOUGHTS & REFLECTIONS

_____

_____

_____

_____

DATE: _____   **Daily Mood Tracker**   DAY: M T W T F S S

TODAY I FEEL

☐ grateful   ☐ motivated   ☐ satisfied   ☐ lonely   ☐ sad   ☐ tired
☐ happy   ☐ productive   ☐ calm   ☐ depressed   ☐ angry   ☐ _____
☐ proud   ☐ relaxed   ☐ powerful   ☐ anxious   ☐ annoyed   ☐ _____

WHY DO I FEEL THIS WAY?

_____

_____

THREE GOALS FOR TODAY

1 _____

2 _____

3 _____

MOOD AM

☺ ☺ ☺ ☹ ☺ ☹ ☹

ENERGY LEVEL AM

1 2 3 4 5 6 7 8 9 10

STRESS LEVEL AM

1 2 3 4 5 6 7 8 9 10

MOOD PM

☺ ☺ ☺ ☹ ☺ ☹ ☹

ENERGY LEVEL PM

1 2 3 4 5 6 7 8 9 10

STRESS LEVEL PM

1 2 3 4 5 6 7 8 9 10

TODAY I HAD

	little	enough
water	☐	☐
fruits	☐	☐
vegetables	☐	☐
sleep	☐	☐
fresh air	☐	☐
free time	☐	☐
	☐	☐

👍 POSITIVE EXPERIENCES TODAY

○ success at work   ○ sports activity
○ meeting with friends   ○ good weather
○ time for family   ○ time in nature
○ excursion   ○ delicious food
○ _____   ○ _____

👎 NEGATIVE EXPERIENCES TODAY

○ failure at work   ○ loneliness
○ dispute   ○ bad weather
○ criticism   ○ bad food
○ exclusion   ○ fears
○ _____   ○ _____

WHAT CAN I DO TO MAKE MY NEXT DAY BETTER?

_____

_____

THOUGHTS & REFLECTIONS

_____

_____

_____

_____

DATE: _____

Daily *Mood* Tracker

DAY: M T W T F S S

TODAY I FEEL

- ☐ grateful
- ☐ happy
- ☐ proud
- ☐ motivated
- ☐ productive
- ☐ relaxed
- ☐ satisfied
- ☐ calm
- ☐ powerful
- ☐ lonely
- ☐ depressed
- ☐ anxious
- ☐ sad
- ☐ angry
- ☐ annoyed
- ☐ tired
- ☐ _____
- ☐ _____

WHY DO I FEEL THIS WAY?

_____

_____

THREE GOALS FOR TODAY

1 _____

2 _____

3 _____

MOOD AM

😄 🙂 😐 🙁 😵 😕 ☹️

ENERGY LEVEL AM

1 2 3 4 5 6 7 8 9 10

STRESS LEVEL AM

1 2 3 4 5 6 7 8 9 10

MOOD PM

😄 🙂 😐 🙁 😵 😕 ☹️

ENERGY LEVEL PM

1 2 3 4 5 6 7 8 9 10

STRESS LEVEL PM

1 2 3 4 5 6 7 8 9 10

TODAY I HAD

	little	enough
water	☐	☐
fruits	☐	☐
vegetables	☐	☐
sleep	☐	☐
fresh air	☐	☐
free time	☐	☐
	☐	☐

👍 POSITIVE EXPERIENCES TODAY

- ○ success at work
- ○ meeting with friends
- ○ time for family
- ○ excursion
- ○ _____
- ○ sports activity
- ○ good weather
- ○ time in nature
- ○ delicious food
- ○ _____

👎 NEGATIVE EXPERIENCES TODAY

- ○ failure at work
- ○ dispute
- ○ criticism
- ○ exclusion
- ○ _____
- ○ loneliness
- ○ bad weather
- ○ bad food
- ○ fears
- ○ _____

WHAT CAN I DO TO MAKE MY NEXT DAY BETTER?

_____

_____

THOUGHTS & REFLECTIONS

_____

_____

_____

_____

DATE: _____   DAY: M T W T F S S

Daily *Mood* Tracker

TODAY I FEEL

☐ grateful   ☐ motivated   ☐ satisfied   ☐ lonely   ☐ sad   ☐ tired
☐ happy   ☐ productive   ☐ calm   ☐ depressed   ☐ angry   ☐ _____
☐ proud   ☐ relaxed   ☐ powerful   ☐ anxious   ☐ annoyed   ☐ _____

WHY DO I FEEL THIS WAY?

_____

_____

THREE GOALS FOR TODAY

1 _____

2 _____

3 _____

MOOD AM

☺ ☺ ☺ ☹ ☹ ☹ ☹

ENERGY LEVEL AM

1 2 3 4 5 6 7 8 9 10

STRESS LEVEL AM

1 2 3 4 5 6 7 8 9 10

MOOD PM

☺ ☺ ☺ ☹ ☹ ☹ ☹

ENERGY LEVEL PM

1 2 3 4 5 6 7 8 9 10

STRESS LEVEL PM

1 2 3 4 5 6 7 8 9 10

TODAY I HAD

	little	enough
water	☐	☐
fruits	☐	☐
vegetables	☐	☐
sleep	☐	☐
fresh air	☐	☐
free time	☐	☐
	☐	☐

👍 POSITIVE EXPERIENCES TODAY

○ success at work   ○ sports activity
○ meeting with friends   ○ good weather
○ time for family   ○ time in nature
○ excursion   ○ delicious food
○ _____   ○ _____

👎 NEGATIVE EXPERIENCES TODAY

○ failure at work   ○ loneliness
○ dispute   ○ bad weather
○ criticism   ○ bad food
○ exclusion   ○ fears
○ _____   ○ _____

WHAT CAN I DO TO MAKE MY NEXT DAY BETTER?

_____

_____

THOUGHTS & REFLECTIONS

_____

_____

_____

_____

DATE: _____   DAY: M T W T F S S

Daily Mood Tracker

TODAY I FEEL

- ☐ grateful
- ☐ happy
- ☐ proud
- ☐ motivated
- ☐ productive
- ☐ relaxed
- ☐ satisfied
- ☐ calm
- ☐ powerful
- ☐ lonely
- ☐ depressed
- ☐ anxious
- ☐ sad
- ☐ angry
- ☐ annoyed
- ☐ tired
- ☐ _____
- ☐ _____

WHY DO I FEEL THIS WAY?

_____

_____

THREE GOALS FOR TODAY

❶ _____

❷ _____

❸ _____

MOOD AM

☺ ☺ ☺ ☹ ☹ ☹ ☹

ENERGY LEVEL AM

1 2 3 4 5 6 7 8 9 10

STRESS LEVEL AM

1 2 3 4 5 6 7 8 9 10

MOOD PM

☺ ☺ ☺ ☹ ☹ ☹ ☹

ENERGY LEVEL PM

1 2 3 4 5 6 7 8 9 10

STRESS LEVEL PM

1 2 3 4 5 6 7 8 9 10

TODAY I HAD

	little	enough
water	☐	☐
fruits	☐	☐
vegetables	☐	☐
sleep	☐	☐
fresh air	☐	☐
free time	☐	☐
	☐	☐

👍 POSITIVE EXPERIENCES TODAY

- ○ success at work
- ○ meeting with friends
- ○ time for family
- ○ excursion
- ○ _____
- ○ sports activity
- ○ good weather
- ○ time in nature
- ○ delicious food
- ○ _____

👎 NEGATIVE EXPERIENCES TODAY

- ○ failure at work
- ○ dispute
- ○ criticism
- ○ exclusion
- ○ _____
- ○ loneliness
- ○ bad weather
- ○ bad food
- ○ fears
- ○ _____

WHAT CAN I DO TO MAKE MY NEXT DAY BETTER?

_____

_____

THOUGHTS & REFLECTIONS

_____

_____

_____

_____

DATE: _____   Daily *Mood* Tracker   DAY: M T W T F S S

TODAY I FEEL

- ☐ grateful
- ☐ happy
- ☐ proud
- ☐ motivated
- ☐ productive
- ☐ relaxed
- ☐ satisfied
- ☐ calm
- ☐ powerful
- ☐ lonely
- ☐ depressed
- ☐ anxious
- ☐ sad
- ☐ angry
- ☐ annoyed
- ☐ tired
- ☐ _____
- ☐ _____

WHY DO I FEEL THIS WAY?

_____

_____

THREE GOALS FOR TODAY

1 _____

2 _____

3 _____

MOOD AM

☺ ☺ ☺ ☹ ☹ ☹ ☹

ENERGY LEVEL AM

1 2 3 4 5 6 7 8 9 10

STRESS LEVEL AM

1 2 3 4 5 6 7 8 9 10

MOOD PM

☺ ☺ ☺ ☹ ☹ ☹ ☹

ENERGY LEVEL PM

1 2 3 4 5 6 7 8 9 10

STRESS LEVEL PM

1 2 3 4 5 6 7 8 9 10

TODAY I HAD

	little	enough
water	☐	☐
fruits	☐	☐
vegetables	☐	☐
sleep	☐	☐
fresh air	☐	☐
free time	☐	☐
	☐	☐

👍 POSITIVE EXPERIENCES TODAY

- ○ success at work
- ○ meeting with friends
- ○ time for family
- ○ excursion
- ○ _____
- ○ sports activity
- ○ good weather
- ○ time in nature
- ○ delicious food
- ○ _____

👎 NEGATIVE EXPERIENCES TODAY

- ○ failure at work
- ○ dispute
- ○ criticism
- ○ exclusion
- ○ _____
- ○ loneliness
- ○ bad weather
- ○ bad food
- ○ fears
- ○ _____

WHAT CAN I DO TO MAKE MY NEXT DAY BETTER?

_____

_____

THOUGHTS & REFLECTIONS

_____

_____

_____

_____

DATE: _____   DAY: M T W T F S S

Daily Mood Tracker

TODAY I FEEL

☐ grateful   ☐ motivated   ☐ satisfied   ☐ lonely   ☐ sad   ☐ tired
☐ happy   ☐ productive   ☐ calm   ☐ depressed   ☐ angry   ☐ _____
☐ proud   ☐ relaxed   ☐ powerful   ☐ anxious   ☐ annoyed   ☐ _____

WHY DO I FEEL THIS WAY?

_____

_____

THREE GOALS FOR TODAY

1 _____

2 _____

3 _____

MOOD AM

☺ ☺ ☺ ☹ ☹ ☹ ☹

ENERGY LEVEL AM

1 2 3 4 5 6 7 8 9 10

STRESS LEVEL AM

1 2 3 4 5 6 7 8 9 10

MOOD PM

☺ ☺ ☺ ☹ ☹ ☹ ☹

ENERGY LEVEL PM

1 2 3 4 5 6 7 8 9 10

STRESS LEVEL PM

1 2 3 4 5 6 7 8 9 10

TODAY I HAD

	little	enough
water	☐	☐
fruits	☐	☐
vegetables	☐	☐
sleep	☐	☐
fresh air	☐	☐
free time	☐	☐
	☐	☐

👍 POSITIVE EXPERIENCES TODAY

○ success at work   ○ sports activity
○ meeting with friends   ○ good weather
○ time for family   ○ time in nature
○ excursion   ○ delicious food
○ _____   ○ _____

👎 NEGATIVE EXPERIENCES TODAY

○ failure at work   ○ loneliness
○ dispute   ○ bad weather
○ criticism   ○ bad food
○ exclusion   ○ fears
○ _____   ○ _____

WHAT CAN I DO TO MAKE MY NEXT DAY BETTER?

_____

_____

THOUGHTS & REFLECTIONS

_____

_____

_____

_____

DATE: _____

Daily *Mood* Tracker

DAY: M T W T F S S

TODAY I FEEL

☐ grateful   ☐ motivated   ☐ satisfied   ☐ lonely   ☐ sad   ☐ tired
☐ happy   ☐ productive   ☐ calm   ☐ depressed   ☐ angry   ☐ _____
☐ proud   ☐ relaxed   ☐ powerful   ☐ anxious   ☐ annoyed   ☐ _____

WHY DO I FEEL THIS WAY?

_____

_____

THREE GOALS FOR TODAY

1 _____

2 _____

3 _____

MOOD AM
😀 🙂 😐 🙁 😣 😟 ☹️

ENERGY LEVEL AM
1 2 3 4 5 6 7 8 9 10

STRESS LEVEL AM
1 2 3 4 5 6 7 8 9 10

MOOD PM
😀 🙂 😐 🙁 😣 😟 ☹️

ENERGY LEVEL PM
1 2 3 4 5 6 7 8 9 10

STRESS LEVEL PM
1 2 3 4 5 6 7 8 9 10

TODAY I HAD

	little	enough
water	☐	☐
fruits	☐	☐
vegetables	☐	☐
sleep	☐	☐
fresh air	☐	☐
free time	☐	☐
	☐	☐

👍 POSITIVE EXPERIENCES TODAY

○ success at work   ○ sports activity
○ meeting with friends   ○ good weather
○ time for family   ○ time in nature
○ excursion   ○ delicious food
○ _____   ○ _____

👎 NEGATIVE EXPERIENCES TODAY

○ failure at work   ○ loneliness
○ dispute   ○ bad weather
○ criticism   ○ bad food
○ exclusion   ○ fears
○ _____   ○ _____

WHAT CAN I DO TO MAKE MY NEXT DAY BETTER?

_____

_____

THOUGHTS & REFLECTIONS

_____

_____

_____

_____

DATE: _____

Daily Mood Tracker

DAY: M T W T F S S

TODAY I FEEL

- ☐ grateful
- ☐ happy
- ☐ proud

- ☐ motivated
- ☐ productive
- ☐ relaxed

- ☐ satisfied
- ☐ calm
- ☐ powerful

- ☐ lonely
- ☐ depressed
- ☐ anxious

- ☐ sad
- ☐ angry
- ☐ annoyed

- ☐ tired
- ☐ _____
- ☐ _____

WHY DO I FEEL THIS WAY?

_____

_____

THREE GOALS FOR TODAY

❶ _____

❷ _____

❸ _____

MOOD AM

😀 🙂 😐 🙁 🤢 😟 ☹️

ENERGY LEVEL AM

1 2 3 4 5 6 7 8 9 10

STRESS LEVEL AM

1 2 3 4 5 6 7 8 9 10

MOOD PM

😀 🙂 😐 🙁 🤢 😟 ☹️

ENERGY LEVEL PM

1 2 3 4 5 6 7 8 9 10

STRESS LEVEL PM

1 2 3 4 5 6 7 8 9 10

TODAY I HAD

	little	enough
water	☐	☐
fruits	☐	☐
vegetables	☐	☐
sleep	☐	☐
fresh air	☐	☐
free time	☐	☐
	☐	☐

👍 POSITIVE EXPERIENCES TODAY

- ○ success at work
- ○ meeting with friends
- ○ time for family
- ○ excursion
- ○ _____

- ○ sports activity
- ○ good weather
- ○ time in nature
- ○ delicious food
- ○ _____

👎 NEGATIVE EXPERIENCES TODAY

- ○ failure at work
- ○ dispute
- ○ criticism
- ○ exclusion
- ○ _____

- ○ loneliness
- ○ bad weather
- ○ bad food
- ○ fears
- ○ _____

WHAT CAN I DO TO MAKE MY NEXT DAY BETTER?

_____

_____

THOUGHTS & REFLECTIONS

_____

_____

_____

_____

DATE: _____   DAY: M T W T F S S

Daily Mood Tracker

TODAY I FEEL

☐ grateful   ☐ motivated   ☐ satisfied   ☐ lonely   ☐ sad   ☐ tired
☐ happy   ☐ productive   ☐ calm   ☐ depressed   ☐ angry   ☐ _____
☐ proud   ☐ relaxed   ☐ powerful   ☐ anxious   ☐ annoyed   ☐ _____

WHY DO I FEEL THIS WAY?

_____

_____

THREE GOALS FOR TODAY

❶ _____

❷ _____

❸ _____

MOOD AM

😀 🙂 😐 🙁 😣 😖 😞

ENERGY LEVEL AM

1 2 3 4 5 6 7 8 9 10

STRESS LEVEL AM

1 2 3 4 5 6 7 8 9 10

MOOD PM

😀 🙂 😐 🙁 😣 😖 😞

ENERGY LEVEL PM

1 2 3 4 5 6 7 8 9 10

STRESS LEVEL PM

1 2 3 4 5 6 7 8 9 10

TODAY I HAD

	little	enough
water	☐	☐
fruits	☐	☐
vegetables	☐	☐
sleep	☐	☐
fresh air	☐	☐
free time	☐	☐
	☐	☐

👍 POSITIVE EXPERIENCES TODAY

○ success at work   ○ sports activity
○ meeting with friends   ○ good weather
○ time for family   ○ time in nature
○ excursion   ○ delicious food
○ _____   ○ _____

👎 NEGATIVE EXPERIENCES TODAY

○ failure at work   ○ loneliness
○ dispute   ○ bad weather
○ criticism   ○ bad food
○ exclusion   ○ fears
○ _____   ○ _____

WHAT CAN I DO TO MAKE MY NEXT DAY BETTER?

_____

_____

THOUGHTS & REFLECTIONS

_____

_____

_____

_____

DATE: _____   DAY: M T W T F S S

Daily Mood Tracker

TODAY I FEEL

- ☐ grateful
- ☐ happy
- ☐ proud
- ☐ motivated
- ☐ productive
- ☐ relaxed
- ☐ satisfied
- ☐ calm
- ☐ powerful
- ☐ lonely
- ☐ depressed
- ☐ anxious
- ☐ sad
- ☐ angry
- ☐ annoyed
- ☐ tired
- ☐ _____
- ☐ _____

WHY DO I FEEL THIS WAY?

_____

_____

THREE GOALS FOR TODAY

❶ _____

❷ _____

❸ _____

MOOD AM
😃 🙂 😐 😕 😟 😣 ☹️

ENERGY LEVEL AM
1 2 3 4 5 6 7 8 9 10

STRESS LEVEL AM
1 2 3 4 5 6 7 8 9 10

MOOD PM
😃 🙂 😐 😕 😟 😣 ☹️

ENERGY LEVEL PM
1 2 3 4 5 6 7 8 9 10

STRESS LEVEL PM
1 2 3 4 5 6 7 8 9 10

TODAY I HAD

	little	enough
water	☐	☐
fruits	☐	☐
vegetables	☐	☐
sleep	☐	☐
fresh air	☐	☐
free time	☐	☐
	☐	☐

👍 POSITIVE EXPERIENCES TODAY

- ○ success at work
- ○ meeting with friends
- ○ time for family
- ○ excursion
- ○ _____
- ○ sports activity
- ○ good weather
- ○ time in nature
- ○ delicious food
- ○ _____

👎 NEGATIVE EXPERIENCES TODAY

- ○ failure at work
- ○ dispute
- ○ criticism
- ○ exclusion
- ○ _____
- ○ loneliness
- ○ bad weather
- ○ bad food
- ○ fears
- ○ _____

WHAT CAN I DO TO MAKE MY NEXT DAY BETTER?

_____

_____

THOUGHTS & REFLECTIONS

_____

_____

_____

_____

DATE: _____   DAY: M T W T F S S

Daily *Mood* Tracker

TODAY I FEEL

☐ grateful   ☐ motivated   ☐ satisfied   ☐ lonely   ☐ sad   ☐ tired
☐ happy   ☐ productive   ☐ calm   ☐ depressed   ☐ angry   ☐ _____
☐ proud   ☐ relaxed   ☐ powerful   ☐ anxious   ☐ annoyed   ☐ _____

WHY DO I FEEL THIS WAY?

_____

_____

THREE GOALS FOR TODAY

① _____

② _____

③ _____

MOOD AM

😃 🙂 😐 🙁 😣 😖 😞

MOOD PM

😃 🙂 😐 🙁 😣 😖 😞

TODAY I HAD

	little	enough
water	☐	☐
fruits	☐	☐
vegetables	☐	☐
sleep	☐	☐
fresh air	☐	☐
free time	☐	☐
	☐	☐

ENERGY LEVEL AM

1 2 3 4 5 6 7 8 9 10

STRESS LEVEL AM

1 2 3 4 5 6 7 8 9 10

ENERGY LEVEL PM

1 2 3 4 5 6 7 8 9 10

STRESS LEVEL PM

1 2 3 4 5 6 7 8 9 10

👍 POSITIVE EXPERIENCES TODAY

○ success at work   ○ sports activity
○ meeting with friends ○ good weather
○ time for family   ○ time in nature
○ excursion   ○ delicious food
○ _____   ○ _____

👎 NEGATIVE EXPERIENCES TODAY

○ failure at work   ○ loneliness
○ dispute   ○ bad weather
○ criticism   ○ bad food
○ exclusion   ○ fears
○ _____   ○ _____

WHAT CAN I DO TO MAKE MY NEXT DAY BETTER?

_____

_____

THOUGHTS & REFLECTIONS

_____

_____

_____

_____

DATE: _____   DAY: M T W T F S S

Daily Mood Tracker

TODAY I FEEL

☐ grateful   ☐ motivated   ☐ satisfied   ☐ lonely   ☐ sad   ☐ tired
☐ happy   ☐ productive   ☐ calm   ☐ depressed   ☐ angry   ☐ _____
☐ proud   ☐ relaxed   ☐ powerful   ☐ anxious   ☐ annoyed ☐ _____

WHY DO I FEEL THIS WAY?

_____

_____

THREE GOALS FOR TODAY

1 _____

2 _____

3 _____

MOOD AM

😁 🙂 😐 🙁 🤢 😖 ☹️

ENERGY LEVEL AM

1 2 3 4 5 6 7 8 9 10

STRESS LEVEL AM

1 2 3 4 5 6 7 8 9 10

MOOD PM

😁 🙂 😐 🙁 🤢 😖 ☹️

ENERGY LEVEL PM

1 2 3 4 5 6 7 8 9 10

STRESS LEVEL PM

1 2 3 4 5 6 7 8 9 10

TODAY I HAD

	little	enough
water	☐	☐
fruits	☐	☐
vegetables	☐	☐
sleep	☐	☐
fresh air	☐	☐
free time	☐	☐
	☐	☐

👍 POSITIVE EXPERIENCES TODAY

○ success at work   ○ sports activity
○ meeting with friends ○ good weather
○ time for family   ○ time in nature
○ excursion   ○ delicious food
○ _____   ○ _____

💬 NEGATIVE EXPERIENCES TODAY

○ failure at work   ○ loneliness
○ dispute   ○ bad weather
○ criticism   ○ bad food
○ exclusion   ○ fears
○ _____   ○ _____

WHAT CAN I DO TO MAKE MY NEXT DAY BETTER?

_____

_____

THOUGHTS & REFLECTIONS

_____

_____

_____

_____

DATE: _____   DAY: M T W T F S S

Daily Mood Tracker

TODAY I FEEL

☐ grateful   ☐ motivated   ☐ satisfied   ☐ lonely   ☐ sad   ☐ tired
☐ happy   ☐ productive   ☐ calm   ☐ depressed   ☐ angry   ☐ _____
☐ proud   ☐ relaxed   ☐ powerful   ☐ anxious   ☐ annoyed   ☐ _____

WHY DO I FEEL THIS WAY?

_____

_____

THREE GOALS FOR TODAY

1 _____

2 _____

3 _____

MOOD AM

😃 🙂 😐 🙁 😓 😕 😖

ENERGY LEVEL AM

1 2 3 4 5 6 7 8 9 10

STRESS LEVEL AM

1 2 3 4 5 6 7 8 9 10

MOOD PM

😃 🙂 😐 🙁 😓 😕 😖

ENERGY LEVEL PM

1 2 3 4 5 6 7 8 9 10

STRESS LEVEL PM

1 2 3 4 5 6 7 8 9 10

TODAY I HAD

	little	enough
water	☐	☐
fruits	☐	☐
vegetables	☐	☐
sleep	☐	☐
fresh air	☐	☐
free time	☐	☐
	☐	☐

👍 POSITIVE EXPERIENCES TODAY

○ success at work   ○ sports activity
○ meeting with friends   ○ good weather
○ time for family   ○ time in nature
○ excursion   ○ delicious food
○ _____   ○ _____

👎 NEGATIVE EXPERIENCES TODAY

○ failure at work   ○ loneliness
○ dispute   ○ bad weather
○ criticism   ○ bad food
○ exclusion   ○ fears
○ _____   ○ _____

WHAT CAN I DO TO MAKE MY NEXT DAY BETTER?

_____

_____

THOUGHTS & REFLECTIONS

_____

_____

_____

_____

DATE: _____   DAY: M T W T F S S

Daily Mood Tracker

TODAY I FEEL

☐ grateful   ☐ motivated   ☐ satisfied   ☐ lonely   ☐ sad   ☐ tired
☐ happy   ☐ productive   ☐ calm   ☐ depressed   ☐ angry   ☐ _____
☐ proud   ☐ relaxed   ☐ powerful   ☐ anxious   ☐ annoyed   ☐ _____

WHY DO I FEEL THIS WAY?

_____

_____

THREE GOALS FOR TODAY

1 _____

2 _____

3 _____

MOOD AM

😄 🙂 😐 🙁 😣 😕 ☹️

ENERGY LEVEL AM

1 2 3 4 5 6 7 8 9 10

STRESS LEVEL AM

1 2 3 4 5 6 7 8 9 10

MOOD PM

😄 🙂 😐 🙁 😣 😕 ☹️

ENERGY LEVEL PM

1 2 3 4 5 6 7 8 9 10

STRESS LEVEL PM

1 2 3 4 5 6 7 8 9 10

TODAY I HAD

	little	enough
water	☐	☐
fruits	☐	☐
vegetables	☐	☐
sleep	☐	☐
fresh air	☐	☐
free time	☐	☐
	☐	☐

👍 POSITIVE EXPERIENCES TODAY

○ success at work   ○ sports activity
○ meeting with friends   ○ good weather
○ time for family   ○ time in nature
○ excursion   ○ delicious food
○ _____   ○ _____

👎 NEGATIVE EXPERIENCES TODAY

○ failure at work   ○ loneliness
○ dispute   ○ bad weather
○ criticism   ○ bad food
○ exclusion   ○ fears
○ _____   ○ _____

WHAT CAN I DO TO MAKE MY NEXT DAY BETTER?

_____

_____

THOUGHTS & REFLECTIONS

_____

_____

_____

_____

DATE: _____ DAY: M T W T F S S

Daily *Mood* Tracker

TODAY I FEEL

☐ grateful ☐ motivated ☐ satisfied ☐ lonely ☐ sad ☐ tired
☐ happy ☐ productive ☐ calm ☐ depressed ☐ angry ☐ _____
☐ proud ☐ relaxed ☐ powerful ☐ anxious ☐ annoyed ☐ _____

WHY DO I FEEL THIS WAY?

_____

_____

THREE GOALS FOR TODAY

1 _____

2 _____

3 _____

MOOD AM

☺ ☺ ☺ ☹ ☹ ☹ ☹

ENERGY LEVEL AM

1 2 3 4 5 6 7 8 9 10

STRESS LEVEL AM

1 2 3 4 5 6 7 8 9 10

MOOD PM

☺ ☺ ☺ ☹ ☹ ☹ ☹

ENERGY LEVEL PM

1 2 3 4 5 6 7 8 9 10

STRESS LEVEL PM

1 2 3 4 5 6 7 8 9 10

TODAY I HAD

	little	enough
water	☐	☐
fruits	☐	☐
vegetables	☐	☐
sleep	☐	☐
fresh air	☐	☐
free time	☐	☐
	☐	☐

👍 POSITIVE EXPERIENCES TODAY

○ success at work   ○ sports activity
○ meeting with friends ○ good weather
○ time for family   ○ time in nature
○ excursion   ○ delicious food
○ _____   ○ _____

👎 NEGATIVE EXPERIENCES TODAY

○ failure at work ○ loneliness
○ dispute   ○ bad weather
○ criticism   ○ bad food
○ exclusion   ○ fears
○ _____ ○ _____

WHAT CAN I DO TO MAKE MY NEXT DAY BETTER?

_____

_____

THOUGHTS & REFLECTIONS

_____

_____

_____

_____

DATE: _____   DAY: M T W T F S S

Daily Mood Tracker

TODAY I FEEL

☐ grateful   ☐ motivated   ☐ satisfied   ☐ lonely   ☐ sad   ☐ tired
☐ happy   ☐ productive   ☐ calm   ☐ depressed   ☐ angry   ☐ _____
☐ proud   ☐ relaxed   ☐ powerful   ☐ anxious   ☐ annoyed   ☐ _____

WHY DO I FEEL THIS WAY?

_____

_____

THREE GOALS FOR TODAY

1 _____

2 _____

3 _____

MOOD AM

😀 🙂 😐 🙁 🥴 😟 😣

ENERGY LEVEL AM

1 2 3 4 5 6 7 8 9 10

STRESS LEVEL AM

1 2 3 4 5 6 7 8 9 10

MOOD PM

😀 🙂 😐 🙁 🥴 😟 😣

ENERGY LEVEL PM

1 2 3 4 5 6 7 8 9 10

STRESS LEVEL PM

1 2 3 4 5 6 7 8 9 10

TODAY I HAD

	little	enough
water	☐	☐
fruits	☐	☐
vegetables	☐	☐
sleep	☐	☐
fresh air	☐	☐
free time	☐	☐
	☐	☐

👍 POSITIVE EXPERIENCES TODAY

○ success at work   ○ sports activity
○ meeting with friends   ○ good weather
○ time for family   ○ time in nature
○ excursion   ○ delicious food
○ _____   ○ _____

💬 NEGATIVE EXPERIENCES TODAY

○ failure at work   ○ loneliness
○ dispute   ○ bad weather
○ criticism   ○ bad food
○ exclusion   ○ fears
○ _____   ○ _____

WHAT CAN I DO TO MAKE MY NEXT DAY BETTER?

_____

_____

THOUGHTS & REFLECTIONS

_____

_____

_____

_____

DATE: _____   DAY: M T W T F S S

Daily *Mood* Tracker

TODAY I FEEL

☐ grateful   ☐ motivated   ☐ satisfied   ☐ lonely   ☐ sad   ☐ tired
☐ happy   ☐ productive   ☐ calm   ☐ depressed   ☐ angry   ☐ _____
☐ proud   ☐ relaxed   ☐ powerful   ☐ anxious   ☐ annoyed   ☐ _____

WHY DO I FEEL THIS WAY?

_____

_____

THREE GOALS FOR TODAY

1 _____

2 _____

3 _____

MOOD AM

☺ ☺ ☺ ☹ ☹ ☹ ☹

ENERGY LEVEL AM

1 2 3 4 5 6 7 8 9 10

STRESS LEVEL AM

1 2 3 4 5 6 7 8 9 10

MOOD PM

☺ ☺ ☺ ☹ ☹ ☹ ☹

ENERGY LEVEL PM

1 2 3 4 5 6 7 8 9 10

STRESS LEVEL PM

1 2 3 4 5 6 7 8 9 10

TODAY I HAD

	little	enough
water	☐	☐
fruits	☐	☐
vegetables	☐	☐
sleep	☐	☐
fresh air	☐	☐
free time	☐	☐
	☐	☐

👍 POSITIVE EXPERIENCES TODAY

○ success at work   ○ sports activity
○ meeting with friends   ○ good weather
○ time for family   ○ time in nature
○ excursion   ○ delicious food
○ _____   ○ _____

👎 NEGATIVE EXPERIENCES TODAY

○ failure at work   ○ loneliness
○ dispute   ○ bad weather
○ criticism   ○ bad food
○ exclusion   ○ fears
○ _____   ○ _____

WHAT CAN I DO TO MAKE MY NEXT DAY BETTER?

_____

_____

THOUGHTS & REFLECTIONS

_____

_____

_____

_____

DATE: _____

Daily Mood Tracker

DAY: M T W T F S S

TODAY I FEEL

☐ grateful   ☐ motivated   ☐ satisfied   ☐ lonely   ☐ sad   ☐ tired
☐ happy   ☐ productive   ☐ calm   ☐ depressed   ☐ angry   ☐ _____
☐ proud   ☐ relaxed   ☐ powerful   ☐ anxious   ☐ annoyed   ☐ _____

WHY DO I FEEL THIS WAY?

_____

_____

THREE GOALS FOR TODAY

1 _____

2 _____

3 _____

MOOD AM

☺ ☺ ☺ ☹ ☹ ☹ ☹

ENERGY LEVEL AM

1 2 3 4 5 6 7 8 9 10

STRESS LEVEL AM

1 2 3 4 5 6 7 8 9 10

MOOD PM

☺ ☺ ☺ ☹ ☹ ☹ ☹

ENERGY LEVEL PM

1 2 3 4 5 6 7 8 9 10

STRESS LEVEL PM

1 2 3 4 5 6 7 8 9 10

TODAY I HAD

	little	enough
water	☐	☐
fruits	☐	☐
vegetables	☐	☐
sleep	☐	☐
fresh air	☐	☐
free time	☐	☐
	☐	☐

👍 POSITIVE EXPERIENCES TODAY

○ success at work   ○ sports activity
○ meeting with friends ○ good weather
○ time for family   ○ time in nature
○ excursion   ○ delicious food
○ _____   ○ _____

👎 NEGATIVE EXPERIENCES TODAY

○ failure at work   ○ loneliness
○ dispute   ○ bad weather
○ criticism   ○ bad food
○ exclusion   ○ fears
○ _____   ○ _____

WHAT CAN I DO TO MAKE MY NEXT DAY BETTER?

_____

_____

THOUGHTS & REFLECTIONS

_____

_____

_____

_____

DATE: _____   DAY: M T W T F S S

Daily *Mood* Tracker

TODAY I FEEL

☐ grateful   ☐ motivated   ☐ satisfied   ☐ lonely   ☐ sad   ☐ tired
☐ happy   ☐ productive   ☐ calm   ☐ depressed   ☐ angry   ☐ _____
☐ proud   ☐ relaxed   ☐ powerful   ☐ anxious   ☐ annoyed   ☐ _____

WHY DO I FEEL THIS WAY?

_____

_____

THREE GOALS FOR TODAY

❶ _____

❷ _____

❸ _____

MOOD AM
😀 🙂 😐 🙁 🥺 😟 😣

ENERGY LEVEL AM
1 2 3 4 5 6 7 8 9 10

STRESS LEVEL AM
1 2 3 4 5 6 7 8 9 10

MOOD PM
😀 🙂 😐 🙁 🥺 😟 😣

ENERGY LEVEL PM
1 2 3 4 5 6 7 8 9 10

STRESS LEVEL PM
1 2 3 4 5 6 7 8 9 10

TODAY I HAD

	little	enough
water	☐	☐
fruits	☐	☐
vegetables	☐	☐
sleep	☐	☐
fresh air	☐	☐
free time	☐	☐
	☐	☐

👍 POSITIVE EXPERIENCES TODAY

○ success at work   ○ sports activity
○ meeting with friends   ○ good weather
○ time for family   ○ time in nature
○ excursion   ○ delicious food
○ _____   ○ _____

👎 NEGATIVE EXPERIENCES TODAY

○ failure at work   ○ loneliness
○ dispute   ○ bad weather
○ criticism   ○ bad food
○ exclusion   ○ fears
○ _____   ○ _____

WHAT CAN I DO TO MAKE MY NEXT DAY BETTER?

_____

_____

THOUGHTS & REFLECTIONS

_____

_____

_____

_____

DATE: _____   DAY: M T W T F S S

Daily Mood Tracker

TODAY I FEEL

☐ grateful   ☐ motivated   ☐ satisfied   ☐ lonely   ☐ sad   ☐ tired
☐ happy   ☐ productive   ☐ calm   ☐ depressed   ☐ angry   ☐ _____
☐ proud   ☐ relaxed   ☐ powerful   ☐ anxious   ☐ annoyed   ☐ _____

WHY DO I FEEL THIS WAY?

_____

_____

THREE GOALS FOR TODAY

❶ _____

❷ _____

❸ _____

MOOD AM	MOOD PM	TODAY I HAD		
😀 🙂 😐 😕 😖 😣 😞	😀 🙂 😐 😕 😖 😣 😞		little	enough
		water	☐	☐
ENERGY LEVEL AM	**ENERGY LEVEL PM**	fruits	☐	☐
1 2 3 4 5 6 7 8 9 10	1 2 3 4 5 6 7 8 9 10	vegetables	☐	☐
		sleep	☐	☐
STRESS LEVEL AM	**STRESS LEVEL PM**	fresh air	☐	☐
1 2 3 4 5 6 7 8 9 10	1 2 3 4 5 6 7 8 9 10	free time	☐	☐
			☐	☐

👍 POSITIVE EXPERIENCES TODAY

○ success at work   ○ sports activity
○ meeting with friends   ○ good weather
○ time for family   ○ time in nature
○ excursion   ○ delicious food
○ _____   ○ _____

💬 NEGATIVE EXPERIENCES TODAY

○ failure at work   ○ loneliness
○ dispute   ○ bad weather
○ criticism   ○ bad food
○ exclusion   ○ fears
○ _____   ○ _____

WHAT CAN I DO TO MAKE MY NEXT DAY BETTER?

_____

_____

THOUGHTS & REFLECTIONS

_____

_____

_____

_____

DATE: _____   Daily *Mood* Tracker   DAY: M T W T F S S

TODAY I FEEL

☐ grateful   ☐ motivated   ☐ satisfied   ☐ lonely   ☐ sad   ☐ tired
☐ happy   ☐ productive   ☐ calm   ☐ depressed   ☐ angry   ☐ _____
☐ proud   ☐ relaxed   ☐ powerful   ☐ anxious   ☐ annoyed ☐ _____

WHY DO I FEEL THIS WAY?

_____

_____

THREE GOALS FOR TODAY

❶ _____

❷ _____

❸ _____

MOOD AM

😀 🙂 😐 🙁 😢 😖 ☹️

ENERGY LEVEL AM

1 2 3 4 5 6 7 8 9 10

STRESS LEVEL AM

1 2 3 4 5 6 7 8 9 10

MOOD PM

😀 🙂 😐 🙁 😢 😖 ☹️

ENERGY LEVEL PM

1 2 3 4 5 6 7 8 9 10

STRESS LEVEL PM

1 2 3 4 5 6 7 8 9 10

TODAY I HAD

	little	enough
water	☐	☐
fruits	☐	☐
vegetables	☐	☐
sleep	☐	☐
fresh air	☐	☐
free time	☐	☐
	☐	☐

👍 POSITIVE EXPERIENCES TODAY

○ success at work   ○ sports activity
○ meeting with friends   ○ good weather
○ time for family   ○ time in nature
○ excursion   ○ delicious food
○ _____   ○ _____

👎 NEGATIVE EXPERIENCES TODAY

○ failure at work   ○ loneliness
○ dispute   ○ bad weather
○ criticism   ○ bad food
○ exclusion   ○ fears
○ _____   ○ _____

WHAT CAN I DO TO MAKE MY NEXT DAY BETTER?

_____

_____

THOUGHTS & REFLECTIONS

_____

_____

_____

_____

DATE: _____   DAY: M T W T F S S

Daily Mood Tracker

TODAY I FEEL

☐ grateful   ☐ motivated   ☐ satisfied   ☐ lonely   ☐ sad   ☐ tired
☐ happy   ☐ productive   ☐ calm   ☐ depressed   ☐ angry   ☐ _____
☐ proud   ☐ relaxed   ☐ powerful   ☐ anxious   ☐ annoyed   ☐ _____

WHY DO I FEEL THIS WAY?

_____

_____

THREE GOALS FOR TODAY

1 _____

2 _____

3 _____

MOOD AM

😃 🙂 😐 🙁 😖 😕 ☹️

ENERGY LEVEL AM

1 2 3 4 5 6 7 8 9 10

STRESS LEVEL AM

1 2 3 4 5 6 7 8 9 10

MOOD PM

😃 🙂 😐 🙁 😖 😕 ☹️

ENERGY LEVEL PM

1 2 3 4 5 6 7 8 9 10

STRESS LEVEL PM

1 2 3 4 5 6 7 8 9 10

TODAY I HAD

	little	enough
water	☐	☐
fruits	☐	☐
vegetables	☐	☐
sleep	☐	☐
fresh air	☐	☐
free time	☐	☐
	☐	☐

👍 POSITIVE EXPERIENCES TODAY

○ success at work   ○ sports activity
○ meeting with friends   ○ good weather
○ time for family   ○ time in nature
○ excursion   ○ delicious food
○ _____   ○ _____

💬 NEGATIVE EXPERIENCES TODAY

○ failure at work   ○ loneliness
○ dispute   ○ bad weather
○ criticism   ○ bad food
○ exclusion   ○ fears
○ _____   ○ _____

WHAT CAN I DO TO MAKE MY NEXT DAY BETTER?

_____

_____

THOUGHTS & REFLECTIONS

_____

_____

_____

_____

DATE: _____   Daily **Mood** Tracker   DAY: M T W T F S S

TODAY I FEEL

- ☐ grateful
- ☐ happy
- ☐ proud
- ☐ motivated
- ☐ productive
- ☐ relaxed
- ☐ satisfied
- ☐ calm
- ☐ powerful
- ☐ lonely
- ☐ depressed
- ☐ anxious
- ☐ sad
- ☐ angry
- ☐ annoyed
- ☐ tired
- ☐ _____
- ☐ _____

WHY DO I FEEL THIS WAY?

_____

_____

THREE GOALS FOR TODAY

❶ _____

❷ _____

❸ _____

MOOD AM

☺ ☺ 😐 ☹ 😓 😖 ☹

ENERGY LEVEL AM

1 2 3 4 5 6 7 8 9 10

STRESS LEVEL AM

1 2 3 4 5 6 7 8 9 10

MOOD PM

☺ ☺ 😐 ☹ 😓 😖 ☹

ENERGY LEVEL PM

1 2 3 4 5 6 7 8 9 10

STRESS LEVEL PM

1 2 3 4 5 6 7 8 9 10

TODAY I HAD

	little	enough
water	☐	☐
fruits	☐	☐
vegetables	☐	☐
sleep	☐	☐
fresh air	☐	☐
free time	☐	☐
	☐	☐

👍 POSITIVE EXPERIENCES TODAY

- ○ success at work
- ○ meeting with friends
- ○ time for family
- ○ excursion
- ○ _____

- ○ sports activity
- ○ good weather
- ○ time in nature
- ○ delicious food
- ○ _____

👎 NEGATIVE EXPERIENCES TODAY

- ○ failure at work
- ○ dispute
- ○ criticism
- ○ exclusion
- ○ _____

- ○ loneliness
- ○ bad weather
- ○ bad food
- ○ fears
- ○ _____

WHAT CAN I DO TO MAKE MY NEXT DAY BETTER?

_____

_____

THOUGHTS & REFLECTIONS

_____

_____

_____

_____

DATE: _____   DAY: M T W T F S S

Daily Mood Tracker

TODAY I FEEL

☐ grateful   ☐ motivated   ☐ satisfied   ☐ lonely   ☐ sad   ☐ tired
☐ happy   ☐ productive   ☐ calm   ☐ depressed   ☐ angry   ☐ _____
☐ proud   ☐ relaxed   ☐ powerful   ☐ anxious   ☐ annoyed   ☐ _____

WHY DO I FEEL THIS WAY?

_____

_____

THREE GOALS FOR TODAY

❶ _____

❷ _____

❸ _____

MOOD AM

😀 🙂 😐 😕 😖 😣 ☹️

ENERGY LEVEL AM

1 2 3 4 5 6 7 8 9 10

STRESS LEVEL AM

1 2 3 4 5 6 7 8 9 10

MOOD PM

😀 🙂 😐 😕 😖 😣 ☹️

ENERGY LEVEL PM

1 2 3 4 5 6 7 8 9 10

STRESS LEVEL PM

1 2 3 4 5 6 7 8 9 10

TODAY I HAD

	little	enough
water	☐	☐
fruits	☐	☐
vegetables	☐	☐
sleep	☐	☐
fresh air	☐	☐
free time	☐	☐
	☐	☐

👍 POSITIVE EXPERIENCES TODAY

○ success at work   ○ sports activity
○ meeting with friends ○ good weather
○ time for family   ○ time in nature
○ excursion   ○ delicious food
○ _____   ○ _____

👎 NEGATIVE EXPERIENCES TODAY

○ failure at work   ○ loneliness
○ dispute   ○ bad weather
○ criticism   ○ bad food
○ exclusion   ○ fears
○ _____   ○ _____

WHAT CAN I DO TO MAKE MY NEXT DAY BETTER?

_____

_____

_____

THOUGHTS & REFLECTIONS

_____

_____

_____

_____

DATE: _____   DAY: M T W T F S S

Daily *Mood* Tracker

TODAY I FEEL

☐ grateful   ☐ motivated   ☐ satisfied   ☐ lonely   ☐ sad   ☐ tired
☐ happy   ☐ productive   ☐ calm   ☐ depressed   ☐ angry   ☐ _____
☐ proud   ☐ relaxed   ☐ powerful   ☐ anxious   ☐ annoyed   ☐ _____

WHY DO I FEEL THIS WAY?

_____

_____

THREE GOALS FOR TODAY

1 _____

2 _____

3 _____

MOOD AM

☺ ☺ ☺ ☹ ☹ ☹ ☹

ENERGY LEVEL AM

1 2 3 4 5 6 7 8 9 10

STRESS LEVEL AM

1 2 3 4 5 6 7 8 9 10

MOOD PM

☺ ☺ ☺ ☹ ☹ ☹ ☹

ENERGY LEVEL PM

1 2 3 4 5 6 7 8 9 10

STRESS LEVEL PM

1 2 3 4 5 6 7 8 9 10

TODAY I HAD

	little	enough
water	☐	☐
fruits	☐	☐
vegetables	☐	☐
sleep	☐	☐
fresh air	☐	☐
free time	☐	☐
	☐	☐

👍 POSITIVE EXPERIENCES TODAY

○ success at work   ○ sports activity
○ meeting with friends   ○ good weather
○ time for family   ○ time in nature
○ excursion   ○ delicious food
○ _____   ○ _____

💬 NEGATIVE EXPERIENCES TODAY

○ failure at work   ○ loneliness
○ dispute   ○ bad weather
○ criticism   ○ bad food
○ exclusion   ○ fears
○ _____   ○ _____

WHAT CAN I DO TO MAKE MY NEXT DAY BETTER?

_____

_____

THOUGHTS & REFLECTIONS

_____

_____

_____

_____

DATE:_____   DAY: M T W T F S S

Daily Mood Tracker

TODAY I FEEL

☐ grateful   ☐ motivated   ☐ satisfied   ☐ lonely   ☐ sad   ☐ tired
☐ happy   ☐ productive   ☐ calm   ☐ depressed   ☐ angry   ☐ _____
☐ proud   ☐ relaxed   ☐ powerful   ☐ anxious   ☐ annoyed   ☐ _____

WHY DO I FEEL THIS WAY?

_____

_____

THREE GOALS FOR TODAY

1 _____

2 _____

3 _____

MOOD AM

😄 🙂 😐 😕 😟 😣 ☹️

ENERGY LEVEL AM

1 2 3 4 5 6 7 8 9 10

STRESS LEVEL AM

1 2 3 4 5 6 7 8 9 10

MOOD PM

😄 🙂 😐 😕 😟 😣 ☹️

ENERGY LEVEL PM

1 2 3 4 5 6 7 8 9 10

STRESS LEVEL PM

1 2 3 4 5 6 7 8 9 10

TODAY I HAD

	little	enough
water	☐	☐
fruits	☐	☐
vegetables	☐	☐
sleep	☐	☐
fresh air	☐	☐
free time	☐	☐
	☐	☐

👍 POSITIVE EXPERIENCES TODAY

○ success at work   ○ sports activity
○ meeting with friends   ○ good weather
○ time for family   ○ time in nature
○ excursion   ○ delicious food
○ _____   ○ _____

👎 NEGATIVE EXPERIENCES TODAY

○ failure at work   ○ loneliness
○ dispute   ○ bad weather
○ criticism   ○ bad food
○ exclusion   ○ fears
○ _____   ○ _____

WHAT CAN I DO TO MAKE MY NEXT DAY BETTER?

_____

_____

THOUGHTS & REFLECTIONS

_____

_____

_____

_____

DATE: _____   Daily **Mood** Tracker   DAY: M T W T F S S

TODAY I FEEL

- ☐ grateful
- ☐ happy
- ☐ proud
- ☐ motivated
- ☐ productive
- ☐ relaxed
- ☐ satisfied
- ☐ calm
- ☐ powerful
- ☐ lonely
- ☐ depressed
- ☐ anxious
- ☐ sad
- ☐ angry
- ☐ annoyed
- ☐ tired
- ☐ _____
- ☐ _____

WHY DO I FEEL THIS WAY?

_____

_____

THREE GOALS FOR TODAY

1 _____

2 _____

3 _____

MOOD AM

☺ ☺ ☺ ☹ ☹ ☹ ☹

ENERGY LEVEL AM

1 2 3 4 5 6 7 8 9 10

STRESS LEVEL AM

1 2 3 4 5 6 7 8 9 10

MOOD PM

☺ ☺ ☺ ☹ ☹ ☹ ☹

ENERGY LEVEL PM

1 2 3 4 5 6 7 8 9 10

STRESS LEVEL PM

1 2 3 4 5 6 7 8 9 10

TODAY I HAD

	little	enough
water	☐	☐
fruits	☐	☐
vegetables	☐	☐
sleep	☐	☐
fresh air	☐	☐
free time	☐	☐
	☐	☐

👍 POSITIVE EXPERIENCES TODAY

- ○ success at work
- ○ meeting with friends
- ○ time for family
- ○ excursion
- ○ _____
- ○ sports activity
- ○ good weather
- ○ time in nature
- ○ delicious food
- ○ _____

💬 NEGATIVE EXPERIENCES TODAY

- ○ failure at work
- ○ dispute
- ○ criticism
- ○ exclusion
- ○ _____
- ○ loneliness
- ○ bad weather
- ○ bad food
- ○ fears
- ○ _____

WHAT CAN I DO TO MAKE MY NEXT DAY BETTER?

_____

_____

THOUGHTS & REFLECTIONS

_____

_____

_____

_____

DATE: _____   DAY: M T W T F S S

Daily *Mood* Tracker

TODAY I FEEL

☐ grateful   ☐ motivated   ☐ satisfied   ☐ lonely   ☐ sad   ☐ tired
☐ happy   ☐ productive   ☐ calm   ☐ depressed   ☐ angry   ☐ _____
☐ proud   ☐ relaxed   ☐ powerful   ☐ anxious   ☐ annoyed   ☐ _____

WHY DO I FEEL THIS WAY?

_____
_____

THREE GOALS FOR TODAY

1 _____

2 _____

3 _____

MOOD AM

☺ ☺ ☺ ☹ ☹ ☹ ☹

ENERGY LEVEL AM

1 2 3 4 5 6 7 8 9 10

STRESS LEVEL AM

1 2 3 4 5 6 7 8 9 10

MOOD PM

☺ ☺ ☺ ☹ ☹ ☹ ☹

ENERGY LEVEL PM

1 2 3 4 5 6 7 8 9 10

STRESS LEVEL PM

1 2 3 4 5 6 7 8 9 10

TODAY I HAD

	little	enough
water	☐	☐
fruits	☐	☐
vegetables	☐	☐
sleep	☐	☐
fresh air	☐	☐
free time	☐	☐
	☐	☐

👍 POSITIVE EXPERIENCES TODAY

○ success at work   ○ sports activity
○ meeting with friends   ○ good weather
○ time for family   ○ time in nature
○ excursion   ○ delicious food
○ _____   ○ _____

💬 NEGATIVE EXPERIENCES TODAY

○ failure at work   ○ loneliness
○ dispute   ○ bad weather
○ criticism   ○ bad food
○ exclusion   ○ fears
○ _____   ○ _____

WHAT CAN I DO TO MAKE MY NEXT DAY BETTER?

_____
_____

THOUGHTS & REFLECTIONS

_____
_____
_____
_____

DATE: _____   Daily *Mood* Tracker   DAY: M T W T F S S

TODAY I FEEL

- ☐ grateful
- ☐ happy
- ☐ proud
- ☐ motivated
- ☐ productive
- ☐ relaxed
- ☐ satisfied
- ☐ calm
- ☐ powerful
- ☐ lonely
- ☐ depressed
- ☐ anxious
- ☐ sad
- ☐ angry
- ☐ annoyed
- ☐ tired
- ☐ _____
- ☐ _____

WHY DO I FEEL THIS WAY?

_____

_____

THREE GOALS FOR TODAY

❶ _____

❷ _____

❸ _____

MOOD AM

😄 🙂 😐 🙁 😔 😟 😣

ENERGY LEVEL AM

1 2 3 4 5 6 7 8 9 10

STRESS LEVEL AM

1 2 3 4 5 6 7 8 9 10

MOOD PM

😄 🙂 😐 🙁 😔 😟 😣

ENERGY LEVEL PM

1 2 3 4 5 6 7 8 9 10

STRESS LEVEL PM

1 2 3 4 5 6 7 8 9 10

TODAY I HAD

	little	enough
water	☐	☐
fruits	☐	☐
vegetables	☐	☐
sleep	☐	☐
fresh air	☐	☐
free time	☐	☐
	☐	☐

👍 POSITIVE EXPERIENCES TODAY

- ○ success at work
- ○ meeting with friends
- ○ time for family
- ○ excursion
- ○ _____
- ○ sports activity
- ○ good weather
- ○ time in nature
- ○ delicious food
- ○ _____

👎 NEGATIVE EXPERIENCES TODAY

- ○ failure at work
- ○ dispute
- ○ criticism
- ○ exclusion
- ○ _____
- ○ loneliness
- ○ bad weather
- ○ bad food
- ○ fears
- ○ _____

WHAT CAN I DO TO MAKE MY NEXT DAY BETTER?

_____

_____

THOUGHTS & REFLECTIONS

_____

_____

_____

_____

DATE: _____

Daily *Mood* Tracker

DAY: M T W T F S S

TODAY I FEEL

☐ grateful   ☐ motivated   ☐ satisfied   ☐ lonely   ☐ sad   ☐ tired
☐ happy   ☐ productive   ☐ calm   ☐ depressed   ☐ angry   ☐ _____
☐ proud   ☐ relaxed   ☐ powerful   ☐ anxious   ☐ annoyed   ☐ _____

WHY DO I FEEL THIS WAY?

_____

_____

THREE GOALS FOR TODAY

1 _____

2 _____

3 _____

MOOD AM

😄 🙂 😐 🙁 😣 😟 😖

ENERGY LEVEL AM

1 2 3 4 5 6 7 8 9 10

STRESS LEVEL AM

1 2 3 4 5 6 7 8 9 10

MOOD PM

😄 🙂 😐 🙁 😣 😟 😖

ENERGY LEVEL PM

1 2 3 4 5 6 7 8 9 10

STRESS LEVEL PM

1 2 3 4 5 6 7 8 9 10

TODAY I HAD

	little	enough
water	☐	☐
fruits	☐	☐
vegetables	☐	☐
sleep	☐	☐
fresh air	☐	☐
free time	☐	☐
	☐	☐

👍 POSITIVE EXPERIENCES TODAY

○ success at work   ○ sports activity
○ meeting with friends   ○ good weather
○ time for family   ○ time in nature
○ excursion   ○ delicious food
○ _____   ○ _____

💬 NEGATIVE EXPERIENCES TODAY

○ failure at work   ○ loneliness
○ dispute   ○ bad weather
○ criticism   ○ bad food
○ exclusion   ○ fears
○ _____   ○ _____

WHAT CAN I DO TO MAKE MY NEXT DAY BETTER?

_____

_____

_____

THOUGHTS & REFLECTIONS

_____

_____

_____

_____

Daily *Mood* Tracker

TODAY I FEEL

- ☐ grateful
- ☐ happy
- ☐ proud
- ☐ motivated
- ☐ productive
- ☐ relaxed
- ☐ satisfied
- ☐ calm
- ☐ powerful
- ☐ lonely
- ☐ depressed
- ☐ anxious
- ☐ sad
- ☐ angry
- ☐ annoyed
- ☐ tired
- ☐ _____
- ☐ _____

WHY DO I FEEL THIS WAY?

_____

_____

THREE GOALS FOR TODAY

1 _____

2 _____

3 _____

MOOD AM

☺ ☺ ☺ ☹ ☹ ☹ ☹

ENERGY LEVEL AM

1 2 3 4 5 6 7 8 9 10

STRESS LEVEL AM

1 2 3 4 5 6 7 8 9 10

MOOD PM

☺ ☺ ☺ ☹ ☹ ☹ ☹

ENERGY LEVEL PM

1 2 3 4 5 6 7 8 9 10

STRESS LEVEL PM

1 2 3 4 5 6 7 8 9 10

TODAY I HAD

	little	enough
water	☐	☐
fruits	☐	☐
vegetables	☐	☐
sleep	☐	☐
fresh air	☐	☐
free time	☐	☐
	☐	☐

👍 POSITIVE EXPERIENCES TODAY

- ○ success at work
- ○ meeting with friends
- ○ time for family
- ○ excursion
- ○ _____
- ○ sports activity
- ○ good weather
- ○ time in nature
- ○ delicious food
- ○ _____

👎 NEGATIVE EXPERIENCES TODAY

- ○ failure at work
- ○ dispute
- ○ criticism
- ○ exclusion
- ○ _____
- ○ loneliness
- ○ bad weather
- ○ bad food
- ○ fears
- ○ _____

WHAT CAN I DO TO MAKE MY NEXT DAY BETTER?

_____

_____

THOUGHTS & REFLECTIONS

_____

_____

_____

_____

DATE: _____   DAY: M T W T F S S

Daily *Mood* Tracker

TODAY I FEEL

☐ grateful   ☐ motivated   ☐ satisfied   ☐ lonely   ☐ sad   ☐ tired
☐ happy   ☐ productive   ☐ calm   ☐ depressed   ☐ angry   ☐ _____
☐ proud   ☐ relaxed   ☐ powerful   ☐ anxious   ☐ annoyed   ☐ _____

WHY DO I FEEL THIS WAY?

_____

_____

THREE GOALS FOR TODAY

❶ _____

❷ _____

❸ _____

MOOD AM

☺ ☺ ☺ ☹ ☹ ☹ ☹

ENERGY LEVEL AM

1 2 3 4 5 6 7 8 9 10

STRESS LEVEL AM

1 2 3 4 5 6 7 8 9 10

MOOD PM

☺ ☺ ☺ ☹ ☹ ☹ ☹

ENERGY LEVEL PM

1 2 3 4 5 6 7 8 9 10

STRESS LEVEL PM

1 2 3 4 5 6 7 8 9 10

TODAY I HAD

	little	enough
water	☐	☐
fruits	☐	☐
vegetables	☐	☐
sleep	☐	☐
fresh air	☐	☐
free time	☐	☐
	☐	☐

👍 POSITIVE EXPERIENCES TODAY

○ success at work   ○ sports activity
○ meeting with friends   ○ good weather
○ time for family   ○ time in nature
○ excursion   ○ delicious food
○ _____   ○ _____

💬 NEGATIVE EXPERIENCES TODAY

○ failure at work   ○ loneliness
○ dispute   ○ bad weather
○ criticism   ○ bad food
○ exclusion   ○ fears
○ _____   ○ _____

WHAT CAN I DO TO MAKE MY NEXT DAY BETTER?

_____

_____

THOUGHTS & REFLECTIONS

_____

_____

_____

_____

DATE: _____   Daily *Mood* Tracker   DAY: M T W T F S S

TODAY I FEEL

☐ grateful   ☐ motivated   ☐ satisfied   ☐ lonely   ☐ sad   ☐ tired
☐ happy   ☐ productive   ☐ calm   ☐ depressed   ☐ angry   ☐ _____
☐ proud   ☐ relaxed   ☐ powerful   ☐ anxious   ☐ annoyed   ☐ _____

WHY DO I FEEL THIS WAY?

_____
_____

THREE GOALS FOR TODAY

❶ _____
❷ _____
❸ _____

MOOD AM

☺ ☺ ☺ ☹ ☹ ☹ ☹

ENERGY LEVEL AM

1 2 3 4 5 6 7 8 9 10

STRESS LEVEL AM

1 2 3 4 5 6 7 8 9 10

MOOD PM

☺ ☺ ☺ ☹ ☹ ☹ ☹

ENERGY LEVEL PM

1 2 3 4 5 6 7 8 9 10

STRESS LEVEL PM

1 2 3 4 5 6 7 8 9 10

TODAY I HAD

	little	enough
water	☐	☐
fruits	☐	☐
vegetables	☐	☐
sleep	☐	☐
fresh air	☐	☐
free time	☐	☐
	☐	☐

👍 POSITIVE EXPERIENCES TODAY

○ success at work   ○ sports activity
○ meeting with friends   ○ good weather
○ time for family   ○ time in nature
○ excursion   ○ delicious food
○ _____   ○ _____

👎 NEGATIVE EXPERIENCES TODAY

○ failure at work   ○ loneliness
○ dispute   ○ bad weather
○ criticism   ○ bad food
○ exclusion   ○ fears
○ _____   ○ _____

WHAT CAN I DO TO MAKE MY NEXT DAY BETTER?

_____
_____
_____

THOUGHTS & REFLECTIONS

_____
_____
_____
_____

DATE: _____   DAY: M T W T F S S

Daily *Mood* Tracker

TODAY I FEEL

☐ grateful	☐ motivated	☐ satisfied	☐ lonely	☐ sad	☐ tired
☐ happy	☐ productive	☐ calm	☐ depressed	☐ angry	☐ _____
☐ proud	☐ relaxed	☐ powerful	☐ anxious	☐ annoyed	☐ _____

WHY DO I FEEL THIS WAY?

_____

_____

THREE GOALS FOR TODAY

❶ _____

❷ _____

❸ _____

MOOD AM

☺ ☺ 😐 ☹ 🥴 😖 ☹

ENERGY LEVEL AM

1 2 3 4 5 6 7 8 9 10

STRESS LEVEL AM

1 2 3 4 5 6 7 8 9 10

MOOD PM

☺ ☺ 😐 ☹ 🥴 😖 ☹

ENERGY LEVEL PM

1 2 3 4 5 6 7 8 9 10

STRESS LEVEL PM

1 2 3 4 5 6 7 8 9 10

TODAY I HAD

	little	enough
water	☐	☐
fruits	☐	☐
vegetables	☐	☐
sleep	☐	☐
fresh air	☐	☐
free time	☐	☐
	☐	☐

👍 POSITIVE EXPERIENCES TODAY

○ success at work	○ sports activity
○ meeting with friends	○ good weather
○ time for family	○ time in nature
○ excursion	○ delicious food
○ _____	○ _____

💬 NEGATIVE EXPERIENCES TODAY

○ failure at work	○ loneliness
○ dispute	○ bad weather
○ criticism	○ bad food
○ exclusion	○ fears
○ _____	○ _____

WHAT CAN I DO TO MAKE MY NEXT DAY BETTER?

_____

_____

THOUGHTS & REFLECTIONS

_____

_____

_____

_____

DATE: _____   Daily *Mood* Tracker   DAY: M T W T F S S

TODAY I FEEL

☐ grateful   ☐ motivated   ☐ satisfied   ☐ lonely   ☐ sad   ☐ tired
☐ happy   ☐ productive   ☐ calm   ☐ depressed   ☐ angry   ☐ _____
☐ proud   ☐ relaxed   ☐ powerful   ☐ anxious   ☐ annoyed   ☐ _____

WHY DO I FEEL THIS WAY?

_____

_____

THREE GOALS FOR TODAY

1 _____

2 _____

3 _____

MOOD AM

😄 🙂 😐 🙁 🥴 😒 😣

ENERGY LEVEL AM

1 2 3 4 5 6 7 8 9 10

STRESS LEVEL AM

1 2 3 4 5 6 7 8 9 10

MOOD PM

😄 🙂 😐 🙁 🥴 😒 😣

ENERGY LEVEL PM

1 2 3 4 5 6 7 8 9 10

STRESS LEVEL PM

1 2 3 4 5 6 7 8 9 10

TODAY I HAD

	little	enough
water	☐	☐
fruits	☐	☐
vegetables	☐	☐
sleep	☐	☐
fresh air	☐	☐
free time	☐	☐
	☐	☐

👍 POSITIVE EXPERIENCES TODAY

○ success at work   ○ sports activity
○ meeting with friends   ○ good weather
○ time for family   ○ time in nature
○ excursion   ○ delicious food
○ _____   ○ _____

👎 NEGATIVE EXPERIENCES TODAY

○ failure at work   ○ loneliness
○ dispute   ○ bad weather
○ criticism   ○ bad food
○ exclusion   ○ fears
○ _____   ○ _____

WHAT CAN I DO TO MAKE MY NEXT DAY BETTER?

_____

_____

THOUGHTS & REFLECTIONS

_____

_____

_____

_____

DATE: _____   DAY: M T W T F S S

Daily Mood Tracker

TODAY I FEEL

☐ grateful   ☐ motivated   ☐ satisfied   ☐ lonely   ☐ sad   ☐ tired
☐ happy   ☐ productive   ☐ calm   ☐ depressed   ☐ angry   ☐ _____
☐ proud   ☐ relaxed   ☐ powerful   ☐ anxious   ☐ annoyed   ☐ _____

WHY DO I FEEL THIS WAY?

_____

_____

THREE GOALS FOR TODAY

1 _____

2 _____

3 _____

MOOD AM
☺ ☺ ☺ ☹ ☹ ☹ ☹

ENERGY LEVEL AM
1 2 3 4 5 6 7 8 9 10

STRESS LEVEL AM
1 2 3 4 5 6 7 8 9 10

MOOD PM
☺ ☺ ☺ ☹ ☹ ☹ ☹

ENERGY LEVEL PM
1 2 3 4 5 6 7 8 9 10

STRESS LEVEL PM
1 2 3 4 5 6 7 8 9 10

TODAY I HAD

	little	enough
water	☐	☐
fruits	☐	☐
vegetables	☐	☐
sleep	☐	☐
fresh air	☐	☐
free time	☐	☐
	☐	☐

👍 POSITIVE EXPERIENCES TODAY

○ success at work   ○ sports activity
○ meeting with friends   ○ good weather
○ time for family   ○ time in nature
○ excursion   ○ delicious food
○ _____   ○ _____

👎 NEGATIVE EXPERIENCES TODAY

○ failure at work   ○ loneliness
○ dispute   ○ bad weather
○ criticism   ○ bad food
○ exclusion   ○ fears
○ _____   ○ _____

WHAT CAN I DO TO MAKE MY NEXT DAY BETTER?

_____

_____

THOUGHTS & REFLECTIONS

_____

_____

_____

_____

DATE: _____   DAY: M T W T F S S

Daily Mood Tracker

TODAY I FEEL

- ☐ grateful
- ☐ happy
- ☐ proud
- ☐ motivated
- ☐ productive
- ☐ relaxed
- ☐ satisfied
- ☐ calm
- ☐ powerful
- ☐ lonely
- ☐ depressed
- ☐ anxious
- ☐ sad
- ☐ angry
- ☐ annoyed
- ☐ tired
- ☐ _____
- ☐ _____

WHY DO I FEEL THIS WAY?

_____

_____

THREE GOALS FOR TODAY

1 _____

2 _____

3 _____

MOOD AM

😀 🙂 😐 🙁 🥺 😞 😣

ENERGY LEVEL AM

1 2 3 4 5 6 7 8 9 10

STRESS LEVEL AM

1 2 3 4 5 6 7 8 9 10

MOOD PM

😀 🙂 😐 🙁 🥺 😞 😣

ENERGY LEVEL PM

1 2 3 4 5 6 7 8 9 10

STRESS LEVEL PM

1 2 3 4 5 6 7 8 9 10

TODAY I HAD

	little	enough
water	☐	☐
fruits	☐	☐
vegetables	☐	☐
sleep	☐	☐
fresh air	☐	☐
free time	☐	☐
	☐	☐

👍 POSITIVE EXPERIENCES TODAY

- ○ success at work
- ○ meeting with friends
- ○ time for family
- ○ excursion
- ○ _____
- ○ sports activity
- ○ good weather
- ○ time in nature
- ○ delicious food
- ○ _____

👎 NEGATIVE EXPERIENCES TODAY

- ○ failure at work
- ○ dispute
- ○ criticism
- ○ exclusion
- ○ _____
- ○ loneliness
- ○ bad weather
- ○ bad food
- ○ fears
- ○ _____

WHAT CAN I DO TO MAKE MY NEXT DAY BETTER?

_____

_____

THOUGHTS & REFLECTIONS

_____

_____

_____

_____

DATE: _____   DAY: M T W T F S S

Daily *Mood* Tracker

TODAY I FEEL

☐ grateful   ☐ motivated   ☐ satisfied   ☐ lonely   ☐ sad   ☐ tired
☐ happy   ☐ productive   ☐ calm   ☐ depressed   ☐ angry   ☐ _____
☐ proud   ☐ relaxed   ☐ powerful   ☐ anxious   ☐ annoyed   ☐ _____

WHY DO I FEEL THIS WAY?

_____

_____

THREE GOALS FOR TODAY

1 _____

2 _____

3 _____

MOOD AM

😆 🙂 😐 😟 😥 😫 😣

ENERGY LEVEL AM

1 2 3 4 5 6 7 8 9 10

STRESS LEVEL AM

1 2 3 4 5 6 7 8 9 10

MOOD PM

😆 🙂 😐 😟 😥 😫 😣

ENERGY LEVEL PM

1 2 3 4 5 6 7 8 9 10

STRESS LEVEL PM

1 2 3 4 5 6 7 8 9 10

TODAY I HAD

	little	enough
water	☐	☐
fruits	☐	☐
vegetables	☐	☐
sleep	☐	☐
fresh air	☐	☐
free time	☐	☐
	☐	☐

👍 POSITIVE EXPERIENCES TODAY

○ success at work   ○ sports activity
○ meeting with friends   ○ good weather
○ time for family   ○ time in nature
○ excursion   ○ delicious food
○ _____   ○ _____

👎 NEGATIVE EXPERIENCES TODAY

○ failure at work   ○ loneliness
○ dispute   ○ bad weather
○ criticism   ○ bad food
○ exclusion   ○ fears
○ _____   ○ _____

WHAT CAN I DO TO MAKE MY NEXT DAY BETTER?

_____

_____

THOUGHTS & REFLECTIONS

_____

_____

_____

_____

DATE: _____   DAY: M T W T F S S

Daily *Mood* Tracker

TODAY I FEEL

☐ grateful   ☐ motivated   ☐ satisfied   ☐ lonely   ☐ sad   ☐ tired
☐ happy   ☐ productive   ☐ calm   ☐ depressed   ☐ angry   ☐ _____
☐ proud   ☐ relaxed   ☐ powerful   ☐ anxious   ☐ annoyed   ☐ _____

WHY DO I FEEL THIS WAY?

_____

_____

THREE GOALS FOR TODAY

❶ _____

❷ _____

❸ _____

MOOD AM

☺ ☺ ☺ ☹ ☹ ☹ ☹

ENERGY LEVEL AM

1 2 3 4 5 6 7 8 9 10

STRESS LEVEL AM

1 2 3 4 5 6 7 8 9 10

MOOD PM

☺ ☺ ☺ ☹ ☹ ☹ ☹

ENERGY LEVEL PM

1 2 3 4 5 6 7 8 9 10

STRESS LEVEL PM

1 2 3 4 5 6 7 8 9 10

TODAY I HAD

	little	enough
water	☐	☐
fruits	☐	☐
vegetables	☐	☐
sleep	☐	☐
fresh air	☐	☐
free time	☐	☐
	☐	☐

👍 POSITIVE EXPERIENCES TODAY

○ success at work   ○ sports activity
○ meeting with friends   ○ good weather
○ time for family   ○ time in nature
○ excursion   ○ delicious food
○ _____   ○ _____

👎 NEGATIVE EXPERIENCES TODAY

○ failure at work   ○ loneliness
○ dispute   ○ bad weather
○ criticism   ○ bad food
○ exclusion   ○ fears
○ _____   ○ _____

WHAT CAN I DO TO MAKE MY NEXT DAY BETTER?

_____

_____

THOUGHTS & REFLECTIONS

_____

_____

_____

_____

DATE: _____   DAY: M T W T F S S

Daily *Mood* Tracker

TODAY I FEEL

- ☐ grateful
- ☐ happy
- ☐ proud
- ☐ motivated
- ☐ productive
- ☐ relaxed
- ☐ satisfied
- ☐ calm
- ☐ powerful
- ☐ lonely
- ☐ depressed
- ☐ anxious
- ☐ sad
- ☐ angry
- ☐ annoyed
- ☐ tired
- ☐ _____
- ☐ _____

WHY DO I FEEL THIS WAY?

_____

_____

THREE GOALS FOR TODAY

❶ _____

❷ _____

❸ _____

MOOD AM

☺ ☺ ☹ ☹ ☹ ☹ ☹

ENERGY LEVEL AM

1 2 3 4 5 6 7 8 9 10

STRESS LEVEL AM

1 2 3 4 5 6 7 8 9 10

MOOD PM

☺ ☺ ☹ ☹ ☹ ☹ ☹

ENERGY LEVEL PM

1 2 3 4 5 6 7 8 9 10

STRESS LEVEL PM

1 2 3 4 5 6 7 8 9 10

TODAY I HAD

	little	enough
water	☐	☐
fruits	☐	☐
vegetables	☐	☐
sleep	☐	☐
fresh air	☐	☐
free time	☐	☐
	☐	☐

👍 POSITIVE EXPERIENCES TODAY

- ○ success at work
- ○ meeting with friends
- ○ time for family
- ○ excursion
- ○ _____
- ○ sports activity
- ○ good weather
- ○ time in nature
- ○ delicious food
- ○ _____

👎 NEGATIVE EXPERIENCES TODAY

- ○ failure at work
- ○ dispute
- ○ criticism
- ○ exclusion
- ○ _____
- ○ loneliness
- ○ bad weather
- ○ bad food
- ○ fears
- ○ _____

WHAT CAN I DO TO MAKE MY NEXT DAY BETTER?

_____

_____

THOUGHTS & REFLECTIONS

_____

_____

_____

_____

DATE: _____   DAY: M T W T F S S

Daily *Mood* Tracker

TODAY I FEEL

☐ grateful   ☐ motivated   ☐ satisfied   ☐ lonely   ☐ sad   ☐ tired
☐ happy   ☐ productive   ☐ calm   ☐ depressed   ☐ angry   ☐ _____
☐ proud   ☐ relaxed   ☐ powerful   ☐ anxious   ☐ annoyed   ☐ _____

WHY DO I FEEL THIS WAY?

_____

_____

THREE GOALS FOR TODAY

1 _____

2 _____

3 _____

MOOD AM

☺ ☺ ☺ ☹ ☺ ☹ ☹

ENERGY LEVEL AM

1 2 3 4 5 6 7 8 9 10

STRESS LEVEL AM

1 2 3 4 5 6 7 8 9 10

MOOD PM

☺ ☺ ☺ ☹ ☺ ☹ ☹

ENERGY LEVEL PM

1 2 3 4 5 6 7 8 9 10

STRESS LEVEL PM

1 2 3 4 5 6 7 8 9 10

TODAY I HAD

	little	enough
water	☐	☐
fruits	☐	☐
vegetables	☐	☐
sleep	☐	☐
fresh air	☐	☐
free time	☐	☐
	☐	☐

👍 POSITIVE EXPERIENCES TODAY

○ success at work   ○ sports activity
○ meeting with friends ○ good weather
○ time for family   ○ time in nature
○ excursion   ○ delicious food
○ _____   ○ _____

👎 NEGATIVE EXPERIENCES TODAY

○ failure at work   ○ loneliness
○ dispute   ○ bad weather
○ criticism   ○ bad food
○ exclusion   ○ fears
○ _____   ○ _____

WHAT CAN I DO TO MAKE MY NEXT DAY BETTER?

_____

_____

THOUGHTS & REFLECTIONS

_____

_____

_____

_____

DATE: _____   DAY: M T W T F S S

Daily Mood Tracker

TODAY I FEEL

- ☐ grateful
- ☐ happy
- ☐ proud
- ☐ motivated
- ☐ productive
- ☐ relaxed
- ☐ satisfied
- ☐ calm
- ☐ powerful
- ☐ lonely
- ☐ depressed
- ☐ anxious
- ☐ sad
- ☐ angry
- ☐ annoyed
- ☐ tired
- ☐ _____
- ☐ _____

WHY DO I FEEL THIS WAY?

_____

_____

THREE GOALS FOR TODAY

1 _____

2 _____

3 _____

MOOD AM

☺ ☺ ☺ ☹ ☹ ☹ ☹

ENERGY LEVEL AM

1 2 3 4 5 6 7 8 9 10

STRESS LEVEL AM

1 2 3 4 5 6 7 8 9 10

MOOD PM

☺ ☺ ☺ ☹ ☹ ☹ ☹

ENERGY LEVEL PM

1 2 3 4 5 6 7 8 9 10

STRESS LEVEL PM

1 2 3 4 5 6 7 8 9 10

TODAY I HAD

	little	enough
water	☐	☐
fruits	☐	☐
vegetables	☐	☐
sleep	☐	☐
fresh air	☐	☐
free time	☐	☐
	☐	☐

👍 POSITIVE EXPERIENCES TODAY

- ○ success at work
- ○ meeting with friends
- ○ time for family
- ○ excursion
- ○ _____
- ○ sports activity
- ○ good weather
- ○ time in nature
- ○ delicious food
- ○ _____

👎 NEGATIVE EXPERIENCES TODAY

- ○ failure at work
- ○ dispute
- ○ criticism
- ○ exclusion
- ○ _____
- ○ loneliness
- ○ bad weather
- ○ bad food
- ○ fears
- ○ _____

WHAT CAN I DO TO MAKE MY NEXT DAY BETTER?

_____

_____

THOUGHTS & REFLECTIONS

_____

_____

_____

_____

DATE: _____   DAY: M T W T F S S

Daily *Mood* Tracker

TODAY I FEEL

- ☐ grateful
- ☐ happy
- ☐ proud
- ☐ motivated
- ☐ productive
- ☐ relaxed
- ☐ satisfied
- ☐ calm
- ☐ powerful
- ☐ lonely
- ☐ depressed
- ☐ anxious
- ☐ sad
- ☐ angry
- ☐ annoyed
- ☐ tired
- ☐ _____
- ☐ _____

WHY DO I FEEL THIS WAY?

_____

_____

THREE GOALS FOR TODAY

1 _____

2 _____

3 _____

MOOD AM

☺ ☺ ☺ ☹ ☺ ☹ ☹

ENERGY LEVEL AM

1 2 3 4 5 6 7 8 9 10

STRESS LEVEL AM

1 2 3 4 5 6 7 8 9 10

MOOD PM

☺ ☺ ☺ ☹ ☺ ☹ ☹

ENERGY LEVEL PM

1 2 3 4 5 6 7 8 9 10

STRESS LEVEL PM

1 2 3 4 5 6 7 8 9 10

TODAY I HAD

	little	enough
water	☐	☐
fruits	☐	☐
vegetables	☐	☐
sleep	☐	☐
fresh air	☐	☐
free time	☐	☐
	☐	☐

👍 POSITIVE EXPERIENCES TODAY

- ○ success at work
- ○ meeting with friends
- ○ time for family
- ○ excursion
- ○ _____
- ○ sports activity
- ○ good weather
- ○ time in nature
- ○ delicious food
- ○ _____

👎 NEGATIVE EXPERIENCES TODAY

- ○ failure at work
- ○ dispute
- ○ criticism
- ○ exclusion
- ○ _____
- ○ loneliness
- ○ bad weather
- ○ bad food
- ○ fears
- ○ _____

WHAT CAN I DO TO MAKE MY NEXT DAY BETTER?

_____

_____

THOUGHTS & REFLECTIONS

_____

_____

_____

_____

DATE: _____   DAY: M T W T F S S

Daily Mood Tracker

TODAY I FEEL

☐ grateful   ☐ motivated   ☐ satisfied   ☐ lonely   ☐ sad   ☐ tired
☐ happy   ☐ productive   ☐ calm   ☐ depressed   ☐ angry   ☐ _____
☐ proud   ☐ relaxed   ☐ powerful   ☐ anxious   ☐ annoyed   ☐ _____

WHY DO I FEEL THIS WAY?

_____

_____

THREE GOALS FOR TODAY

1 _____

2 _____

3 _____

MOOD AM

☺ ☺ 😐 🙁 😕 😟 ☹

ENERGY LEVEL AM

1 2 3 4 5 6 7 8 9 10

STRESS LEVEL AM

1 2 3 4 5 6 7 8 9 10

MOOD PM

☺ ☺ 😐 🙁 😕 😟 ☹

ENERGY LEVEL PM

1 2 3 4 5 6 7 8 9 10

STRESS LEVEL PM

1 2 3 4 5 6 7 8 9 10

TODAY I HAD

	little	enough
water	☐	☐
fruits	☐	☐
vegetables	☐	☐
sleep	☐	☐
fresh air	☐	☐
free time	☐	☐
	☐	☐

👍 POSITIVE EXPERIENCES TODAY

○ success at work   ○ sports activity
○ meeting with friends ○ good weather
○ time for family   ○ time in nature
○ excursion   ○ delicious food
○ _____   ○ _____

👎 NEGATIVE EXPERIENCES TODAY

○ failure at work   ○ loneliness
○ dispute   ○ bad weather
○ criticism   ○ bad food
○ exclusion   ○ fears
○ _____   ○ _____

WHAT CAN I DO TO MAKE MY NEXT DAY BETTER?

_____

_____

THOUGHTS & REFLECTIONS

_____

_____

_____

_____

DATE: _____   **Daily** *Mood* **Tracker**   DAY: M T W T F S S

TODAY I FEEL

☐ grateful   ☐ motivated   ☐ satisfied   ☐ lonely   ☐ sad   ☐ tired
☐ happy   ☐ productive   ☐ calm   ☐ depressed   ☐ angry   ☐ _____
☐ proud   ☐ relaxed   ☐ powerful   ☐ anxious   ☐ annoyed   ☐ _____

WHY DO I FEEL THIS WAY?

_____

_____

THREE GOALS FOR TODAY

❶ _____

❷ _____

❸ _____

MOOD AM

☺ ☺ 😐 ☹ 😕 😬 ☹

ENERGY LEVEL AM

1 2 3 4 5 6 7 8 9 10

STRESS LEVEL AM

1 2 3 4 5 6 7 8 9 10

MOOD PM

☺ ☺ 😐 ☹ 😕 😬 ☹

ENERGY LEVEL PM

1 2 3 4 5 6 7 8 9 10

STRESS LEVEL PM

1 2 3 4 5 6 7 8 9 10

TODAY I HAD

	little	enough
water	☐	☐
fruits	☐	☐
vegetables	☐	☐
sleep	☐	☐
fresh air	☐	☐
free time	☐	☐
	☐	☐

👍 POSITIVE EXPERIENCES TODAY

○ success at work   ○ sports activity
○ meeting with friends   ○ good weather
○ time for family   ○ time in nature
○ excursion   ○ delicious food
○ _____   ○ _____

👎 NEGATIVE EXPERIENCES TODAY

○ failure at work   ○ loneliness
○ dispute   ○ bad weather
○ criticism   ○ bad food
○ exclusion   ○ fears
○ _____   ○ _____

WHAT CAN I DO TO MAKE MY NEXT DAY BETTER?

_____

_____

THOUGHTS & REFLECTIONS

_____

_____

_____

_____

DATE: _____

Daily *Mood* Tracker

DAY: M T W T F S S

TODAY I FEEL

- ☐ grateful
- ☐ happy
- ☐ proud
- ☐ motivated
- ☐ productive
- ☐ relaxed
- ☐ satisfied
- ☐ calm
- ☐ powerful
- ☐ lonely
- ☐ depressed
- ☐ anxious
- ☐ sad
- ☐ angry
- ☐ annoyed
- ☐ tired
- ☐ _____
- ☐ _____

WHY DO I FEEL THIS WAY?

_____

_____

THREE GOALS FOR TODAY

1 _____

2 _____

3 _____

MOOD AM

☺ ☺ ☺ ☹ ☹ ☹ ☹

ENERGY LEVEL AM
1 2 3 4 5 6 7 8 9 10

STRESS LEVEL AM
1 2 3 4 5 6 7 8 9 10

MOOD PM

☺ ☺ ☺ ☹ ☹ ☹ ☹

ENERGY LEVEL PM
1 2 3 4 5 6 7 8 9 10

STRESS LEVEL PM
1 2 3 4 5 6 7 8 9 10

TODAY I HAD

	little	enough
water	☐	☐
fruits	☐	☐
vegetables	☐	☐
sleep	☐	☐
fresh air	☐	☐
free time	☐	☐
	☐	☐

👍 POSITIVE EXPERIENCES TODAY

- ○ success at work
- ○ meeting with friends
- ○ time for family
- ○ excursion
- ○ _____
- ○ sports activity
- ○ good weather
- ○ time in nature
- ○ delicious food
- ○ _____

💬 NEGATIVE EXPERIENCES TODAY

- ○ failure at work
- ○ dispute
- ○ criticism
- ○ exclusion
- ○ _____
- ○ loneliness
- ○ bad weather
- ○ bad food
- ○ fears
- ○ _____

WHAT CAN I DO TO MAKE MY NEXT DAY BETTER?

_____

_____

THOUGHTS & REFLECTIONS

_____

_____

_____

_____

DATE: _____   Daily *Mood* Tracker   DAY: M T W T F S S

TODAY I FEEL

☐ grateful   ☐ motivated   ☐ satisfied   ☐ lonely   ☐ sad   ☐ tired
☐ happy   ☐ productive   ☐ calm   ☐ depressed ☐ angry   ☐ _____
☐ proud   ☐ relaxed   ☐ powerful   ☐ anxious   ☐ annoyed   ☐ _____

WHY DO I FEEL THIS WAY?

_____

_____

THREE GOALS FOR TODAY

❶ _____

❷ _____

❸ _____

MOOD AM
😄 🙂 😐 🙁 😫 😕 ☹️

ENERGY LEVEL AM
1 2 3 4 5 6 7 8 9 10

STRESS LEVEL AM
1 2 3 4 5 6 7 8 9 10

MOOD PM
😄 🙂 😐 🙁 😫 😕 ☹️

ENERGY LEVEL PM
1 2 3 4 5 6 7 8 9 10

STRESS LEVEL PM
1 2 3 4 5 6 7 8 9 10

TODAY I HAD

	little	enough
water	☐	☐
fruits	☐	☐
vegetables	☐	☐
sleep	☐	☐
fresh air	☐	☐
free time	☐	☐
	☐	☐

👍 POSITIVE EXPERIENCES TODAY

○ success at work   ○ sports activity
○ meeting with friends   ○ good weather
○ time for family   ○ time in nature
○ excursion   ○ delicious food
○ _____   ○ _____

👎 NEGATIVE EXPERIENCES TODAY

○ failure at work   ○ loneliness
○ dispute   ○ bad weather
○ criticism   ○ bad food
○ exclusion   ○ fears
○ _____   ○ _____

WHAT CAN I DO TO MAKE MY NEXT DAY BETTER?

_____

_____

_____

THOUGHTS & REFLECTIONS

_____

_____

_____

_____

DATE: _____   DAY: M T W T F S S

Daily Mood Tracker

TODAY I FEEL

- ☐ grateful
- ☐ happy
- ☐ proud

- ☐ motivated
- ☐ productive
- ☐ relaxed

- ☐ satisfied
- ☐ calm
- ☐ powerful

- ☐ lonely
- ☐ depressed
- ☐ anxious

- ☐ sad
- ☐ angry
- ☐ annoyed

- ☐ tired
- ☐ _____
- ☐ _____

WHY DO I FEEL THIS WAY?

_____

_____

THREE GOALS FOR TODAY

1 _____

2 _____

3 _____

MOOD AM

😄 🙂 😐 🙁 😵 😖 😣

ENERGY LEVEL AM

1 2 3 4 5 6 7 8 9 10

STRESS LEVEL AM

1 2 3 4 5 6 7 8 9 10

MOOD PM

😄 🙂 😐 🙁 😵 😖 😣

ENERGY LEVEL PM

1 2 3 4 5 6 7 8 9 10

STRESS LEVEL PM

1 2 3 4 5 6 7 8 9 10

TODAY I HAD

	little	enough
water	☐	☐
fruits	☐	☐
vegetables	☐	☐
sleep	☐	☐
fresh air	☐	☐
free time	☐	☐
	☐	☐

👍 POSITIVE EXPERIENCES TODAY

- ○ success at work
- ○ meeting with friends
- ○ time for family
- ○ excursion
- ○ _____

- ○ sports activity
- ○ good weather
- ○ time in nature
- ○ delicious food
- ○ _____

👎 NEGATIVE EXPERIENCES TODAY

- ○ failure at work
- ○ dispute
- ○ criticism
- ○ exclusion
- ○ _____

- ○ loneliness
- ○ bad weather
- ○ bad food
- ○ fears
- ○ _____

WHAT CAN I DO TO MAKE MY NEXT DAY BETTER?

_____

_____

THOUGHTS & REFLECTIONS

_____

_____

_____

_____

DATE: _____   DAY: M T W T F S S

Daily *Mood* Tracker

TODAY I FEEL

☐ grateful	☐ motivated	☐ satisfied	☐ lonely	☐ sad	☐ tired
☐ happy	☐ productive	☐ calm	☐ depressed	☐ angry	☐ _____
☐ proud	☐ relaxed	☐ powerful	☐ anxious	☐ annoyed	☐ _____

WHY DO I FEEL THIS WAY?

_____

_____

THREE GOALS FOR TODAY

❶ _____

❷ _____

❸ _____

MOOD AM

😀 🙂 😐 🙁 😓 😑 ☹️

ENERGY LEVEL AM
1 2 3 4 5 6 7 8 9 10

STRESS LEVEL AM
1 2 3 4 5 6 7 8 9 10

MOOD PM

😀 🙂 😐 🙁 😓 😑 ☹️

ENERGY LEVEL PM
1 2 3 4 5 6 7 8 9 10

STRESS LEVEL PM
1 2 3 4 5 6 7 8 9 10

TODAY I HAD

	little	enough
water	☐	☐
fruits	☐	☐
vegetables	☐	☐
sleep	☐	☐
fresh air	☐	☐
free time	☐	☐
	☐	☐

👍 POSITIVE EXPERIENCES TODAY

○ success at work	○ sports activity
○ meeting with friends	○ good weather
○ time for family	○ time in nature
○ excursion	○ delicious food
○ _____	○ _____

👎 NEGATIVE EXPERIENCES TODAY

○ failure at work	○ loneliness
○ dispute	○ bad weather
○ criticism	○ bad food
○ exclusion	○ fears
○ _____	○ _____

WHAT CAN I DO TO MAKE MY NEXT DAY BETTER?

_____

_____

THOUGHTS & REFLECTIONS

_____

_____

_____

_____

DATE: _____   DAY: M T W T F S S

Daily Mood Tracker

TODAY I FEEL

☐ grateful   ☐ motivated   ☐ satisfied   ☐ lonely   ☐ sad   ☐ tired
☐ happy   ☐ productive   ☐ calm   ☐ depressed   ☐ angry   ☐ _____
☐ proud   ☐ relaxed   ☐ powerful   ☐ anxious   ☐ annoyed   ☐ _____

WHY DO I FEEL THIS WAY?

_____

_____

THREE GOALS FOR TODAY

1 _____

2 _____

3 _____

MOOD AM

😄 🙂 😐 😕 😣 😟 ☹️

ENERGY LEVEL AM

1 2 3 4 5 6 7 8 9 10

STRESS LEVEL AM

1 2 3 4 5 6 7 8 9 10

MOOD PM

😄 🙂 😐 😕 😣 😟 ☹️

ENERGY LEVEL PM

1 2 3 4 5 6 7 8 9 10

STRESS LEVEL PM

1 2 3 4 5 6 7 8 9 10

TODAY I HAD

	little	enough
water	☐	☐
fruits	☐	☐
vegetables	☐	☐
sleep	☐	☐
fresh air	☐	☐
free time	☐	☐
	☐	☐

👍 POSITIVE EXPERIENCES TODAY

○ success at work   ○ sports activity
○ meeting with friends   ○ good weather
○ time for family   ○ time in nature
○ excursion   ○ delicious food
○ _____   ○ _____

👎 NEGATIVE EXPERIENCES TODAY

○ failure at work   ○ loneliness
○ dispute   ○ bad weather
○ criticism   ○ bad food
○ exclusion   ○ fears
○ _____   ○ _____

WHAT CAN I DO TO MAKE MY NEXT DAY BETTER?

_____

_____

THOUGHTS & REFLECTIONS

_____

_____

_____

_____

DATE: _____　　　　　　　　　　　　　　　　DAY: M T W T F S S

Daily Mood Tracker

TODAY I FEEL

- ☐ grateful
- ☐ happy
- ☐ proud
- ☐ motivated
- ☐ productive
- ☐ relaxed
- ☐ satisfied
- ☐ calm
- ☐ powerful
- ☐ lonely
- ☐ depressed
- ☐ anxious
- ☐ sad
- ☐ angry
- ☐ annoyed
- ☐ tired
- ☐ _____
- ☐ _____

WHY DO I FEEL THIS WAY?

_____

_____

THREE GOALS FOR TODAY

❶ _____

❷ _____

❸ _____

MOOD AM

☺ ☺ 😐 ☹ 😖 😑 ☹

ENERGY LEVEL AM

1 2 3 4 5 6 7 8 9 10

STRESS LEVEL AM

1 2 3 4 5 6 7 8 9 10

MOOD PM

☺ ☺ 😐 ☹ 😖 😑 ☹

ENERGY LEVEL PM

1 2 3 4 5 6 7 8 9 10

STRESS LEVEL PM

1 2 3 4 5 6 7 8 9 10

TODAY I HAD

	little	enough
water	☐	☐
fruits	☐	☐
vegetables	☐	☐
sleep	☐	☐
fresh air	☐	☐
free time	☐	☐
	☐	☐

👍 POSITIVE EXPERIENCES TODAY

- ○ success at work
- ○ meeting with friends
- ○ time for family
- ○ excursion
- ○ _____
- ○ sports activity
- ○ good weather
- ○ time in nature
- ○ delicious food
- ○ _____

👎 NEGATIVE EXPERIENCES TODAY

- ○ failure at work
- ○ dispute
- ○ criticism
- ○ exclusion
- ○ _____
- ○ loneliness
- ○ bad weather
- ○ bad food
- ○ fears
- ○ _____

WHAT CAN I DO TO MAKE MY NEXT DAY BETTER?

_____

_____

THOUGHTS & REFLECTIONS

_____

_____

_____

_____

DATE: _____   DAY: M T W T F S S

Daily Mood Tracker

TODAY I FEEL

☐ grateful ☐ motivated ☐ satisfied ☐ lonely ☐ sad ☐ tired
☐ happy ☐ productive ☐ calm ☐ depressed ☐ angry ☐ _____
☐ proud ☐ relaxed ☐ powerful ☐ anxious ☐ annoyed ☐ _____

WHY DO I FEEL THIS WAY?

_____

_____

THREE GOALS FOR TODAY

1 _____

2 _____

3 _____

MOOD AM

😃 🙂 😐 🙁 😣 😟 ☹️

MOOD PM

😃 🙂 😐 🙁 😣 😟 ☹️

TODAY I HAD

	little	enough
water	☐	☐
fruits	☐	☐
vegetables	☐	☐
sleep	☐	☐
fresh air	☐	☐
free time	☐	☐
	☐	☐

ENERGY LEVEL AM

1 2 3 4 5 6 7 8 9 10

STRESS LEVEL AM

1 2 3 4 5 6 7 8 9 10

ENERGY LEVEL PM

1 2 3 4 5 6 7 8 9 10

STRESS LEVEL PM

1 2 3 4 5 6 7 8 9 10

👍 POSITIVE EXPERIENCES TODAY

○ success at work   ○ sports activity
○ meeting with friends   ○ good weather
○ time for family   ○ time in nature
○ excursion   ○ delicious food
○ _____   ○ _____

👎 NEGATIVE EXPERIENCES TODAY

○ failure at work   ○ loneliness
○ dispute   ○ bad weather
○ criticism   ○ bad food
○ exclusion   ○ fears
○ _____   ○ _____

WHAT CAN I DO TO MAKE MY NEXT DAY BETTER?

_____

_____

THOUGHTS & REFLECTIONS

_____

_____

_____

_____

DATE: _____   DAY: M T W T F S S

Daily Mood Tracker

TODAY I FEEL

☐ grateful   ☐ motivated   ☐ satisfied   ☐ lonely   ☐ sad   ☐ tired
☐ happy   ☐ productive   ☐ calm   ☐ depressed   ☐ angry   ☐ _____
☐ proud   ☐ relaxed   ☐ powerful   ☐ anxious   ☐ annoyed   ☐ _____

WHY DO I FEEL THIS WAY?

_____

_____

THREE GOALS FOR TODAY

❶ _____

❷ _____

❸ _____

MOOD AM
☺ ☺ ☺ ☹ ☹ ☹ ☹

ENERGY LEVEL AM
1 2 3 4 5 6 7 8 9 10

STRESS LEVEL AM
1 2 3 4 5 6 7 8 9 10

MOOD PM
☺ ☺ ☺ ☹ ☹ ☹ ☹

ENERGY LEVEL PM
1 2 3 4 5 6 7 8 9 10

STRESS LEVEL PM
1 2 3 4 5 6 7 8 9 10

TODAY I HAD

	little	enough
water	☐	☐
fruits	☐	☐
vegetables	☐	☐
sleep	☐	☐
fresh air	☐	☐
free time	☐	☐
	☐	☐

👍 POSITIVE EXPERIENCES TODAY

○ success at work   ○ sports activity
○ meeting with friends   ○ good weather
○ time for family   ○ time in nature
○ excursion   ○ delicious food
○ _____   ○ _____

💬 NEGATIVE EXPERIENCES TODAY

○ failure at work   ○ loneliness
○ dispute   ○ bad weather
○ criticism   ○ bad food
○ exclusion   ○ fears
○ _____   ○ _____

WHAT CAN I DO TO MAKE MY NEXT DAY BETTER?

_____

_____

THOUGHTS & REFLECTIONS

_____

_____

_____

_____

DATE: _____   DAY: M T W T F S S

Daily *Mood* Tracker

TODAY I FEEL

- ☐ grateful
- ☐ happy
- ☐ proud
- ☐ motivated
- ☐ productive
- ☐ relaxed
- ☐ satisfied
- ☐ calm
- ☐ powerful
- ☐ lonely
- ☐ depressed
- ☐ anxious
- ☐ sad
- ☐ angry
- ☐ annoyed
- ☐ tired
- ☐ _____
- ☐ _____

WHY DO I FEEL THIS WAY?

_____

_____

THREE GOALS FOR TODAY

1 _____

2 _____

3 _____

MOOD AM

😄 🙂 😐 😕 🥴 😣 😖

ENERGY LEVEL AM

1 2 3 4 5 6 7 8 9 10

STRESS LEVEL AM

1 2 3 4 5 6 7 8 9 10

MOOD PM

😄 🙂 😐 😕 🥴 😣 😖

ENERGY LEVEL PM

1 2 3 4 5 6 7 8 9 10

STRESS LEVEL PM

1 2 3 4 5 6 7 8 9 10

TODAY I HAD

	little	enough
water	☐	☐
fruits	☐	☐
vegetables	☐	☐
sleep	☐	☐
fresh air	☐	☐
free time	☐	☐
	☐	☐

👍 POSITIVE EXPERIENCES TODAY

- ○ success at work
- ○ meeting with friends
- ○ time for family
- ○ excursion
- ○ _____
- ○ sports activity
- ○ good weather
- ○ time in nature
- ○ delicious food
- ○ _____

💬 NEGATIVE EXPERIENCES TODAY

- ○ failure at work
- ○ dispute
- ○ criticism
- ○ exclusion
- ○ _____
- ○ loneliness
- ○ bad weather
- ○ bad food
- ○ fears
- ○ _____

WHAT CAN I DO TO MAKE MY NEXT DAY BETTER?

_____

_____

THOUGHTS & REFLECTIONS

_____

_____

_____

_____

DATE: _____

Daily *Mood* Tracker

DAY: M T W T F S S

TODAY I FEEL

- ☐ grateful
- ☐ happy
- ☐ proud
- ☐ motivated
- ☐ productive
- ☐ relaxed
- ☐ satisfied
- ☐ calm
- ☐ powerful
- ☐ lonely
- ☐ depressed
- ☐ anxious
- ☐ sad
- ☐ angry
- ☐ annoyed
- ☐ tired
- ☐ _____
- ☐ _____

WHY DO I FEEL THIS WAY?

_____

_____

THREE GOALS FOR TODAY

1 _____

2 _____

3 _____

MOOD AM

😀 🙂 😐 🙁 😟 😕 ☹️

ENERGY LEVEL AM

1 2 3 4 5 6 7 8 9 10

STRESS LEVEL AM

1 2 3 4 5 6 7 8 9 10

MOOD PM

😀 🙂 😐 🙁 😟 😕 ☹️

ENERGY LEVEL PM

1 2 3 4 5 6 7 8 9 10

STRESS LEVEL PM

1 2 3 4 5 6 7 8 9 10

TODAY I HAD

	little	enough
water	☐	☐
fruits	☐	☐
vegetables	☐	☐
sleep	☐	☐
fresh air	☐	☐
free time	☐	☐
	☐	☐

👍 POSITIVE EXPERIENCES TODAY

- ○ success at work
- ○ meeting with friends
- ○ time for family
- ○ excursion
- ○ _____
- ○ sports activity
- ○ good weather
- ○ time in nature
- ○ delicious food
- ○ _____

💬 NEGATIVE EXPERIENCES TODAY

- ○ failure at work
- ○ dispute
- ○ criticism
- ○ exclusion
- ○ _____
- ○ loneliness
- ○ bad weather
- ○ bad food
- ○ fears
- ○ _____

WHAT CAN I DO TO MAKE MY NEXT DAY BETTER?

_____

_____

THOUGHTS & REFLECTIONS

_____

_____

_____

_____

DATE: _____   DAY: M T W T F S S

Daily *Mood* Tracker

TODAY I FEEL

- ☐ grateful
- ☐ happy
- ☐ proud
- ☐ motivated
- ☐ productive
- ☐ relaxed
- ☐ satisfied
- ☐ calm
- ☐ powerful
- ☐ lonely
- ☐ depressed
- ☐ anxious
- ☐ sad
- ☐ angry
- ☐ annoyed
- ☐ tired
- ☐ _____
- ☐ _____

WHY DO I FEEL THIS WAY?

_____

_____

THREE GOALS FOR TODAY

❶ _____

❷ _____

❸ _____

MOOD AM

☺ ☺ ☺ ☹ ☹ ☹ ☹

ENERGY LEVEL AM

1 2 3 4 5 6 7 8 9 10

STRESS LEVEL AM

1 2 3 4 5 6 7 8 9 10

MOOD PM

☺ ☺ ☺ ☹ ☹ ☹ ☹

ENERGY LEVEL PM

1 2 3 4 5 6 7 8 9 10

STRESS LEVEL PM

1 2 3 4 5 6 7 8 9 10

TODAY I HAD

	little	enough
water	☐	☐
fruits	☐	☐
vegetables	☐	☐
sleep	☐	☐
fresh air	☐	☐
free time	☐	☐
	☐	☐

👍 POSITIVE EXPERIENCES TODAY

- ○ success at work
- ○ meeting with friends
- ○ time for family
- ○ excursion
- ○ _____
- ○ sports activity
- ○ good weather
- ○ time in nature
- ○ delicious food
- ○ _____

💬 NEGATIVE EXPERIENCES TODAY

- ○ failure at work
- ○ dispute
- ○ criticism
- ○ exclusion
- ○ _____
- ○ loneliness
- ○ bad weather
- ○ bad food
- ○ fears
- ○ _____

WHAT CAN I DO TO MAKE MY NEXT DAY BETTER?

_____

_____

THOUGHTS & REFLECTIONS

_____

_____

_____

_____

DATE: _____   DAY: M T W T F S S

Daily Mood Tracker

TODAY I FEEL

☐ grateful   ☐ motivated   ☐ satisfied   ☐ lonely   ☐ sad   ☐ tired
☐ happy   ☐ productive   ☐ calm   ☐ depressed   ☐ angry   ☐ _____
☐ proud   ☐ relaxed   ☐ powerful   ☐ anxious   ☐ annoyed   ☐ _____

WHY DO I FEEL THIS WAY?

_____

_____

THREE GOALS FOR TODAY

❶ _____

❷ _____

❸ _____

MOOD AM

😀 🙂 😐 🙁 😟 😞 😣

ENERGY LEVEL AM

1 2 3 4 5 6 7 8 9 10

STRESS LEVEL AM

1 2 3 4 5 6 7 8 9 10

MOOD PM

😀 🙂 😐 🙁 😟 😞 😣

ENERGY LEVEL PM

1 2 3 4 5 6 7 8 9 10

STRESS LEVEL PM

1 2 3 4 5 6 7 8 9 10

TODAY I HAD

	little	enough
water	☐	☐
fruits	☐	☐
vegetables	☐	☐
sleep	☐	☐
fresh air	☐	☐
free time	☐	☐
	☐	☐

👍 POSITIVE EXPERIENCES TODAY

○ success at work   ○ sports activity
○ meeting with friends   ○ good weather
○ time for family   ○ time in nature
○ excursion   ○ delicious food
○ _____   ○ _____

👎 NEGATIVE EXPERIENCES TODAY

○ failure at work   ○ loneliness
○ dispute   ○ bad weather
○ criticism   ○ bad food
○ exclusion   ○ fears
○ _____   ○ _____

WHAT CAN I DO TO MAKE MY NEXT DAY BETTER?

_____

_____

THOUGHTS & REFLECTIONS

_____

_____

_____

_____

DATE: _____

Daily *Mood* Tracker

DAY: M T W T F S S

TODAY I FEEL

- ☐ grateful
- ☐ happy
- ☐ proud
- ☐ motivated
- ☐ productive
- ☐ relaxed
- ☐ satisfied
- ☐ calm
- ☐ powerful
- ☐ lonely
- ☐ depressed
- ☐ anxious
- ☐ sad
- ☐ angry
- ☐ annoyed
- ☐ tired
- ☐ _____
- ☐ _____

WHY DO I FEEL THIS WAY?

_____

_____

THREE GOALS FOR TODAY

1 _____

2 _____

3 _____

MOOD AM

☺ ☺ 😐 ☹ 😰 😕 ☹

ENERGY LEVEL AM

1 2 3 4 5 6 7 8 9 10

STRESS LEVEL AM

1 2 3 4 5 6 7 8 9 10

MOOD PM

☺ ☺ 😐 ☹ 😰 😕 ☹

ENERGY LEVEL PM

1 2 3 4 5 6 7 8 9 10

STRESS LEVEL PM

1 2 3 4 5 6 7 8 9 10

TODAY I HAD

	little	enough
water	☐	☐
fruits	☐	☐
vegetables	☐	☐
sleep	☐	☐
fresh air	☐	☐
free time	☐	☐
	☐	☐

👍 POSITIVE EXPERIENCES TODAY

- ○ success at work
- ○ meeting with friends
- ○ time for family
- ○ excursion
- ○ _____
- ○ sports activity
- ○ good weather
- ○ time in nature
- ○ delicious food
- ○ _____

👎 NEGATIVE EXPERIENCES TODAY

- ○ failure at work
- ○ dispute
- ○ criticism
- ○ exclusion
- ○ _____
- ○ loneliness
- ○ bad weather
- ○ bad food
- ○ fears
- ○ _____

WHAT CAN I DO TO MAKE MY NEXT DAY BETTER?

_____

_____

THOUGHTS & REFLECTIONS

_____

_____

_____

_____

DATE: _____   DAY: M T W T F S S

Daily *Mood* Tracker

TODAY I FEEL

☐ grateful   ☐ motivated   ☐ satisfied   ☐ lonely   ☐ sad   ☐ tired
☐ happy   ☐ productive   ☐ calm   ☐ depressed   ☐ angry   ☐ _____
☐ proud   ☐ relaxed   ☐ powerful   ☐ anxious   ☐ annoyed   ☐ _____

WHY DO I FEEL THIS WAY?

_____

_____

THREE GOALS FOR TODAY

1 _____

2 _____

3 _____

MOOD AM

☺ ☺ ☺ ☺ ☺ ☺ ☹

ENERGY LEVEL AM

1 2 3 4 5 6 7 8 9 10

STRESS LEVEL AM

1 2 3 4 5 6 7 8 9 10

MOOD PM

☺ ☺ ☺ ☺ ☺ ☺ ☹

ENERGY LEVEL PM

1 2 3 4 5 6 7 8 9 10

STRESS LEVEL PM

1 2 3 4 5 6 7 8 9 10

TODAY I HAD

	little	enough
water	☐	☐
fruits	☐	☐
vegetables	☐	☐
sleep	☐	☐
fresh air	☐	☐
free time	☐	☐
	☐	☐

👍 POSITIVE EXPERIENCES TODAY

○ success at work   ○ sports activity
○ meeting with friends ○ good weather
○ time for family   ○ time in nature
○ excursion   ○ delicious food
○ _____   ○ _____

💬 NEGATIVE EXPERIENCES TODAY

○ failure at work   ○ loneliness
○ dispute   ○ bad weather
○ criticism   ○ bad food
○ exclusion   ○ fears
○ _____   ○ _____

WHAT CAN I DO TO MAKE MY NEXT DAY BETTER?

_____

_____

THOUGHTS & REFLECTIONS

_____

_____

_____

_____

DATE: _____

Daily Mood Tracker

DAY: M T W T F S S

TODAY I FEEL

- ☐ grateful
- ☐ happy
- ☐ proud
- ☐ motivated
- ☐ productive
- ☐ relaxed
- ☐ satisfied
- ☐ calm
- ☐ powerful
- ☐ lonely
- ☐ depressed
- ☐ anxious
- ☐ sad
- ☐ angry
- ☐ annoyed
- ☐ tired
- ☐ _____
- ☐ _____

WHY DO I FEEL THIS WAY?

_____

_____

THREE GOALS FOR TODAY

1 _____

2 _____

3 _____

MOOD AM

😀 🙂 😐 😕 😣 😟 😣

ENERGY LEVEL AM

1 2 3 4 5 6 7 8 9 10

STRESS LEVEL AM

1 2 3 4 5 6 7 8 9 10

MOOD PM

😀 🙂 😐 😕 😣 😟 😣

ENERGY LEVEL PM

1 2 3 4 5 6 7 8 9 10

STRESS LEVEL PM

1 2 3 4 5 6 7 8 9 10

TODAY I HAD

	little	enough
water	☐	☐
fruits	☐	☐
vegetables	☐	☐
sleep	☐	☐
fresh air	☐	☐
free time	☐	☐
	☐	☐

👍 POSITIVE EXPERIENCES TODAY

- ○ success at work
- ○ meeting with friends
- ○ time for family
- ○ excursion
- ○ _____
- ○ sports activity
- ○ good weather
- ○ time in nature
- ○ delicious food
- ○ _____

👎 NEGATIVE EXPERIENCES TODAY

- ○ failure at work
- ○ dispute
- ○ criticism
- ○ exclusion
- ○ _____
- ○ loneliness
- ○ bad weather
- ○ bad food
- ○ fears
- ○ _____

WHAT CAN I DO TO MAKE MY NEXT DAY BETTER?

_____

_____

THOUGHTS & REFLECTIONS

_____

_____

_____

_____

DATE: _____   DAY: M T W T F S S

Daily *Mood* Tracker

TODAY I FEEL

☐ grateful	☐ motivated	☐ satisfied	☐ lonely	☐ sad	☐ tired
☐ happy	☐ productive	☐ calm	☐ depressed	☐ angry	☐ _____
☐ proud	☐ relaxed	☐ powerful	☐ anxious	☐ annoyed	☐ _____

WHY DO I FEEL THIS WAY?

_____

_____

THREE GOALS FOR TODAY

1 _____

2 _____

3 _____

MOOD AM

☺ ☺ ☺ ☹ ☹ ☹ ☹

ENERGY LEVEL AM

1 2 3 4 5 6 7 8 9 10

STRESS LEVEL AM

1 2 3 4 5 6 7 8 9 10

MOOD PM

☺ ☺ ☺ ☹ ☹ ☹ ☹

ENERGY LEVEL PM

1 2 3 4 5 6 7 8 9 10

STRESS LEVEL PM

1 2 3 4 5 6 7 8 9 10

TODAY I HAD

	little	enough
water	☐	☐
fruits	☐	☐
vegetables	☐	☐
sleep	☐	☐
fresh air	☐	☐
free time	☐	☐
	☐	☐

👍 POSITIVE EXPERIENCES TODAY

○ success at work	○ sports activity
○ meeting with friends	○ good weather
○ time for family	○ time in nature
○ excursion	○ delicious food
○ _____	○ _____

👎 NEGATIVE EXPERIENCES TODAY

○ failure at work	○ loneliness
○ dispute	○ bad weather
○ criticism	○ bad food
○ exclusion	○ fears
○ _____	○ _____

WHAT CAN I DO TO MAKE MY NEXT DAY BETTER?

_____

_____

THOUGHTS & REFLECTIONS

_____

_____

_____

_____

DATE: _____

Daily *Mood* Tracker

DAY: M T W T F S S

TODAY I FEEL

☐ grateful   ☐ motivated   ☐ satisfied   ☐ lonely   ☐ sad   ☐ tired
☐ happy   ☐ productive   ☐ calm   ☐ depressed   ☐ angry   ☐ _____
☐ proud   ☐ relaxed   ☐ powerful   ☐ anxious   ☐ annoyed   ☐ _____

WHY DO I FEEL THIS WAY?

_____

_____

THREE GOALS FOR TODAY

1 _____

2 _____

3 _____

MOOD AM

☺ ☺ ☺ ☹ ☹ ☹ ☹

ENERGY LEVEL AM

1 2 3 4 5 6 7 8 9 10

STRESS LEVEL AM

1 2 3 4 5 6 7 8 9 10

MOOD PM

☺ ☺ ☺ ☹ ☹ ☹ ☹

ENERGY LEVEL PM

1 2 3 4 5 6 7 8 9 10

STRESS LEVEL PM

1 2 3 4 5 6 7 8 9 10

TODAY I HAD

	little	enough
water	☐	☐
fruits	☐	☐
vegetables	☐	☐
sleep	☐	☐
fresh air	☐	☐
free time	☐	☐
	☐	☐

👍 POSITIVE EXPERIENCES TODAY

○ success at work   ○ sports activity
○ meeting with friends   ○ good weather
○ time for family   ○ time in nature
○ excursion   ○ delicious food
○ _____   ○ _____

👎 NEGATIVE EXPERIENCES TODAY

○ failure at work   ○ loneliness
○ dispute   ○ bad weather
○ criticism   ○ bad food
○ exclusion   ○ fears
○ _____   ○ _____

WHAT CAN I DO TO MAKE MY NEXT DAY BETTER?

_____

_____

THOUGHTS & REFLECTIONS

_____

_____

_____

_____

DATE: _____   DAY: M T W T F S S

Daily Mood Tracker

TODAY I FEEL

☐ grateful   ☐ motivated   ☐ satisfied   ☐ lonely   ☐ sad   ☐ tired
☐ happy   ☐ productive   ☐ calm   ☐ depressed   ☐ angry   ☐ _____
☐ proud   ☐ relaxed   ☐ powerful   ☐ anxious   ☐ annoyed   ☐ _____

WHY DO I FEEL THIS WAY?

_____

_____

THREE GOALS FOR TODAY

❶ _____

❷ _____

❸ _____

MOOD AM

😄 🙂 😐 🙁 😟 😖 ☹️

ENERGY LEVEL AM

1 2 3 4 5 6 7 8 9 10

STRESS LEVEL AM

1 2 3 4 5 6 7 8 9 10

MOOD PM

😄 🙂 😐 🙁 😟 😖 ☹️

ENERGY LEVEL PM

1 2 3 4 5 6 7 8 9 10

STRESS LEVEL PM

1 2 3 4 5 6 7 8 9 10

TODAY I HAD

	little	enough
water	☐	☐
fruits	☐	☐
vegetables	☐	☐
sleep	☐	☐
fresh air	☐	☐
free time	☐	☐
	☐	☐

👍 POSITIVE EXPERIENCES TODAY

○ success at work   ○ sports activity
○ meeting with friends ○ good weather
○ time for family   ○ time in nature
○ excursion   ○ delicious food
○ _____   ○ _____

👎 NEGATIVE EXPERIENCES TODAY

○ failure at work   ○ loneliness
○ dispute   ○ bad weather
○ criticism   ○ bad food
○ exclusion   ○ fears
○ _____   ○ _____

WHAT CAN I DO TO MAKE MY NEXT DAY BETTER?

_____

_____

THOUGHTS & REFLECTIONS

_____

_____

_____

_____

DATE:_____ Daily *Mood* Tracker DAY: M T W T F S S

TODAY I FEEL

- ☐ grateful
- ☐ happy
- ☐ proud
- ☐ motivated
- ☐ productive
- ☐ relaxed
- ☐ satisfied
- ☐ calm
- ☐ powerful
- ☐ lonely
- ☐ depressed
- ☐ anxious
- ☐ sad
- ☐ angry
- ☐ annoyed
- ☐ tired
- ☐ _____
- ☐ _____

WHY DO I FEEL THIS WAY?

_____
_____

THREE GOALS FOR TODAY

1 _____

2 _____

3 _____

MOOD AM

😀 🙂 😐 🙁 😖 😔 ☹️

ENERGY LEVEL AM

1 2 3 4 5 6 7 8 9 10

STRESS LEVEL AM

1 2 3 4 5 6 7 8 9 10

MOOD PM

😀 🙂 😐 🙁 😖 😔 ☹️

ENERGY LEVEL PM

1 2 3 4 5 6 7 8 9 10

STRESS LEVEL PM

1 2 3 4 5 6 7 8 9 10

TODAY I HAD

	little	enough
water	☐	☐
fruits	☐	☐
vegetables	☐	☐
sleep	☐	☐
fresh air	☐	☐
free time	☐	☐
	☐	☐

👍 POSITIVE EXPERIENCES TODAY

- ○ success at work
- ○ meeting with friends
- ○ time for family
- ○ excursion
- ○ _____
- ○ sports activity
- ○ good weather
- ○ time in nature
- ○ delicious food
- ○ _____

💬 NEGATIVE EXPERIENCES TODAY

- ○ failure at work
- ○ dispute
- ○ criticism
- ○ exclusion
- ○ _____
- ○ loneliness
- ○ bad weather
- ○ bad food
- ○ fears
- ○ _____

WHAT CAN I DO TO MAKE MY NEXT DAY BETTER?

_____
_____

THOUGHTS & REFLECTIONS

_____
_____
_____
_____

DATE: _____   DAY: M T W T F S S

Daily *Mood* Tracker

TODAY I FEEL

☐ grateful   ☐ motivated   ☐ satisfied   ☐ lonely   ☐ sad   ☐ tired
☐ happy   ☐ productive   ☐ calm   ☐ depressed   ☐ angry   ☐ _____
☐ proud   ☐ relaxed   ☐ powerful   ☐ anxious   ☐ annoyed   ☐ _____

WHY DO I FEEL THIS WAY?

_____

_____

THREE GOALS FOR TODAY

❶ _____

❷ _____

❸ _____

MOOD AM

☺ ☺ ☺ ☹ ☹ ☹ ☹

ENERGY LEVEL AM

1 2 3 4 5 6 7 8 9 10

STRESS LEVEL AM

1 2 3 4 5 6 7 8 9 10

MOOD PM

☺ ☺ ☺ ☹ ☹ ☹ ☹

ENERGY LEVEL PM

1 2 3 4 5 6 7 8 9 10

STRESS LEVEL PM

1 2 3 4 5 6 7 8 9 10

TODAY I HAD

	little	enough
water	☐	☐
fruits	☐	☐
vegetables	☐	☐
sleep	☐	☐
fresh air	☐	☐
free time	☐	☐
	☐	☐

👍 POSITIVE EXPERIENCES TODAY

○ success at work   ○ sports activity
○ meeting with friends   ○ good weather
○ time for family   ○ time in nature
○ excursion   ○ delicious food
○ _____   ○ _____

👎 NEGATIVE EXPERIENCES TODAY

○ failure at work   ○ loneliness
○ dispute   ○ bad weather
○ criticism   ○ bad food
○ exclusion   ○ fears
○ _____   ○ _____

WHAT CAN I DO TO MAKE MY NEXT DAY BETTER?

_____

_____

THOUGHTS & REFLECTIONS

_____

_____

_____

_____

DATE: _____   DAY: M T W T F S S

Daily *Mood* Tracker

TODAY I FEEL

- ☐ grateful
- ☐ happy
- ☐ proud
- ☐ motivated
- ☐ productive
- ☐ relaxed
- ☐ satisfied
- ☐ calm
- ☐ powerful
- ☐ lonely
- ☐ depressed
- ☐ anxious
- ☐ sad
- ☐ angry
- ☐ annoyed
- ☐ tired
- ☐ _____
- ☐ _____

WHY DO I FEEL THIS WAY?

_____

_____

THREE GOALS FOR TODAY

1 _____

2 _____

3 _____

MOOD AM

☺ ☺ ☺ ☹ ☹ ☹ ☹

ENERGY LEVEL AM

1 2 3 4 5 6 7 8 9 10

STRESS LEVEL AM

1 2 3 4 5 6 7 8 9 10

MOOD PM

☺ ☺ ☺ ☹ ☹ ☹ ☹

ENERGY LEVEL PM

1 2 3 4 5 6 7 8 9 10

STRESS LEVEL PM

1 2 3 4 5 6 7 8 9 10

TODAY I HAD

	little	enough
water	☐	☐
fruits	☐	☐
vegetables	☐	☐
sleep	☐	☐
fresh air	☐	☐
free time	☐	☐
	☐	☐

👍 POSITIVE EXPERIENCES TODAY

- ○ success at work
- ○ meeting with friends
- ○ time for family
- ○ excursion
- ○ _____
- ○ sports activity
- ○ good weather
- ○ time in nature
- ○ delicious food
- ○ _____

💬 NEGATIVE EXPERIENCES TODAY

- ○ failure at work
- ○ dispute
- ○ criticism
- ○ exclusion
- ○ _____
- ○ loneliness
- ○ bad weather
- ○ bad food
- ○ fears
- ○ _____

WHAT CAN I DO TO MAKE MY NEXT DAY BETTER?

_____

_____

THOUGHTS & REFLECTIONS

_____

_____

_____

_____

DATE: _____   DAY: M T W T F S S

Daily *Mood* Tracker

TODAY I FEEL

- ☐ grateful
- ☐ happy
- ☐ proud
- ☐ motivated
- ☐ productive
- ☐ relaxed
- ☐ satisfied
- ☐ calm
- ☐ powerful
- ☐ lonely
- ☐ depressed
- ☐ anxious
- ☐ sad
- ☐ angry
- ☐ annoyed
- ☐ tired
- ☐ _____
- ☐ _____

WHY DO I FEEL THIS WAY?

_____

_____

THREE GOALS FOR TODAY

1. _____
2. _____
3. _____

MOOD AM

😄 🙂 😐 🙁 😟 😒 ☹️

ENERGY LEVEL AM

1 2 3 4 5 6 7 8 9 10

STRESS LEVEL AM

1 2 3 4 5 6 7 8 9 10

MOOD PM

😄 🙂 😐 🙁 😟 😒 ☹️

ENERGY LEVEL PM

1 2 3 4 5 6 7 8 9 10

STRESS LEVEL PM

1 2 3 4 5 6 7 8 9 10

TODAY I HAD

	little	enough
water	☐	☐
fruits	☐	☐
vegetables	☐	☐
sleep	☐	☐
fresh air	☐	☐
free time	☐	☐
	☐	☐

👍 POSITIVE EXPERIENCES TODAY

- ○ success at work
- ○ meeting with friends
- ○ time for family
- ○ excursion
- ○ _____
- ○ sports activity
- ○ good weather
- ○ time in nature
- ○ delicious food
- ○ _____

💬 NEGATIVE EXPERIENCES TODAY

- ○ failure at work
- ○ dispute
- ○ criticism
- ○ exclusion
- ○ _____
- ○ loneliness
- ○ bad weather
- ○ bad food
- ○ fears
- ○ _____

WHAT CAN I DO TO MAKE MY NEXT DAY BETTER?

_____

_____

THOUGHTS & REFLECTIONS

_____

_____

_____

_____

DATE: _____   DAY: M T W T F S S

Daily *Mood* Tracker

TODAY I FEEL

- ☐ grateful
- ☐ happy
- ☐ proud
- ☐ motivated
- ☐ productive
- ☐ relaxed
- ☐ satisfied
- ☐ calm
- ☐ powerful
- ☐ lonely
- ☐ depressed
- ☐ anxious
- ☐ sad
- ☐ angry
- ☐ annoyed
- ☐ tired
- ☐ _____
- ☐ _____

WHY DO I FEEL THIS WAY?

_____

_____

THREE GOALS FOR TODAY

1 _____

2 _____

3 _____

MOOD AM

☺ ☺ ☺ ☹ ☹ ☹ ☹

ENERGY LEVEL AM

1 2 3 4 5 6 7 8 9 10

STRESS LEVEL AM

1 2 3 4 5 6 7 8 9 10

MOOD PM

☺ ☺ ☺ ☹ ☹ ☹ ☹

ENERGY LEVEL PM

1 2 3 4 5 6 7 8 9 10

STRESS LEVEL PM

1 2 3 4 5 6 7 8 9 10

TODAY I HAD

	little	enough
water	☐	☐
fruits	☐	☐
vegetables	☐	☐
sleep	☐	☐
fresh air	☐	☐
free time	☐	☐
	☐	☐

👍 POSITIVE EXPERIENCES TODAY

- ○ success at work
- ○ meeting with friends
- ○ time for family
- ○ excursion
- ○ _____
- ○ sports activity
- ○ good weather
- ○ time in nature
- ○ delicious food
- ○ _____

👎 NEGATIVE EXPERIENCES TODAY

- ○ failure at work
- ○ dispute
- ○ criticism
- ○ exclusion
- ○ _____
- ○ loneliness
- ○ bad weather
- ○ bad food
- ○ fears
- ○ _____

WHAT CAN I DO TO MAKE MY NEXT DAY BETTER?

_____

_____

THOUGHTS & REFLECTIONS

_____

_____

_____

_____

DATE: _____

Daily Mood Tracker

DAY: M T W T F S S

TODAY I FEEL

☐ grateful   ☐ motivated   ☐ satisfied   ☐ lonely   ☐ sad   ☐ tired
☐ happy   ☐ productive   ☐ calm   ☐ depressed   ☐ angry   ☐ _____
☐ proud   ☐ relaxed   ☐ powerful   ☐ anxious   ☐ annoyed   ☐ _____

WHY DO I FEEL THIS WAY?

_____

_____

THREE GOALS FOR TODAY

❶ _____

❷ _____

❸ _____

MOOD AM

😄 🙂 😐 🙁 😟 😖 😣

ENERGY LEVEL AM

1 2 3 4 5 6 7 8 9 10

STRESS LEVEL AM

1 2 3 4 5 6 7 8 9 10

MOOD PM

😄 🙂 😐 🙁 😟 😖 😣

ENERGY LEVEL PM

1 2 3 4 5 6 7 8 9 10

STRESS LEVEL PM

1 2 3 4 5 6 7 8 9 10

TODAY I HAD

	little	enough
water	☐	☐
fruits	☐	☐
vegetables	☐	☐
sleep	☐	☐
fresh air	☐	☐
free time	☐	☐
	☐	☐

👍 POSITIVE EXPERIENCES TODAY

○ success at work   ○ sports activity
○ meeting with friends   ○ good weather
○ time for family   ○ time in nature
○ excursion   ○ delicious food
○ _____   ○ _____

💬 NEGATIVE EXPERIENCES TODAY

○ failure at work   ○ loneliness
○ dispute   ○ bad weather
○ criticism   ○ bad food
○ exclusion   ○ fears
○ _____   ○ _____

WHAT CAN I DO TO MAKE MY NEXT DAY BETTER?

_____

_____

THOUGHTS & REFLECTIONS

_____

_____

_____

_____

DATE: _____

Daily *Mood* Tracker

DAY: M T W T F S S

TODAY I FEEL

☐ grateful   ☐ motivated   ☐ satisfied   ☐ lonely   ☐ sad   ☐ tired
☐ happy   ☐ productive   ☐ calm   ☐ depressed   ☐ angry   ☐ _____
☐ proud   ☐ relaxed   ☐ powerful   ☐ anxious   ☐ annoyed   ☐ _____

WHY DO I FEEL THIS WAY?

_____

_____

THREE GOALS FOR TODAY

1 _____

2 _____

3 _____

MOOD AM

☺ ☺ ☺ ☹ ☹ ☹ ☹

ENERGY LEVEL AM

1 2 3 4 5 6 7 8 9 10

STRESS LEVEL AM

1 2 3 4 5 6 7 8 9 10

MOOD PM

☺ ☺ ☺ ☹ ☹ ☹ ☹

ENERGY LEVEL PM

1 2 3 4 5 6 7 8 9 10

STRESS LEVEL PM

1 2 3 4 5 6 7 8 9 10

TODAY I HAD

	little	enough
water	☐	☐
fruits	☐	☐
vegetables	☐	☐
sleep	☐	☐
fresh air	☐	☐
free time	☐	☐
	☐	☐

👍 POSITIVE EXPERIENCES TODAY

○ success at work   ○ sports activity
○ meeting with friends ○ good weather
○ time for family   ○ time in nature
○ excursion   ○ delicious food
○ _____   ○ _____

👎 NEGATIVE EXPERIENCES TODAY

○ failure at work   ○ loneliness
○ dispute   ○ bad weather
○ criticism   ○ bad food
○ exclusion   ○ fears
○ _____   ○ _____

WHAT CAN I DO TO MAKE MY NEXT DAY BETTER?

_____

_____

THOUGHTS & REFLECTIONS

_____

_____

_____

_____

DATE: _____   DAY: M T W T F S S

Daily *Mood* Tracker

TODAY I FEEL

☐ grateful   ☐ motivated   ☐ satisfied   ☐ lonely   ☐ sad   ☐ tired
☐ happy   ☐ productive   ☐ calm   ☐ depressed ☐ angry   ☐ _____
☐ proud   ☐ relaxed   ☐ powerful   ☐ anxious   ☐ annoyed ☐ _____

WHY DO I FEEL THIS WAY?

_____

_____

THREE GOALS FOR TODAY

1 _____

2 _____

3 _____

MOOD AM

☺ ☺ ☺ ☺ ☺ ☺ ☹

ENERGY LEVEL AM

1 2 3 4 5 6 7 8 9 10

STRESS LEVEL AM

1 2 3 4 5 6 7 8 9 10

MOOD PM

☺ ☺ ☺ ☺ ☺ ☺ ☹

ENERGY LEVEL PM

1 2 3 4 5 6 7 8 9 10

STRESS LEVEL PM

1 2 3 4 5 6 7 8 9 10

TODAY I HAD

	little	enough
water	☐	☐
fruits	☐	☐
vegetables	☐	☐
sleep	☐	☐
fresh air	☐	☐
free time	☐	☐
	☐	☐

👍 POSITIVE EXPERIENCES TODAY

○ success at work   ○ sports activity
○ meeting with friends ○ good weather
○ time for family   ○ time in nature
○ excursion   ○ delicious food
○ _____   ○ _____

👎 NEGATIVE EXPERIENCES TODAY

○ failure at work   ○ loneliness
○ dispute   ○ bad weather
○ criticism   ○ bad food
○ exclusion   ○ fears
○ _____   ○ _____

WHAT CAN I DO TO MAKE MY NEXT DAY BETTER?

_____

_____

THOUGHTS & REFLECTIONS

_____

_____

_____

_____

DATE: _____   *Daily* **Mood** Tracker   DAY: M T W T F S S

TODAY I FEEL

☐ grateful   ☐ motivated   ☐ satisfied   ☐ lonely   ☐ sad   ☐ tired
☐ happy   ☐ productive   ☐ calm   ☐ depressed   ☐ angry   ☐ _____
☐ proud   ☐ relaxed   ☐ powerful   ☐ anxious   ☐ annoyed   ☐ _____

WHY DO I FEEL THIS WAY?

_____

_____

THREE GOALS FOR TODAY

1 _____

2 _____

3 _____

MOOD AM
😄 🙂 😐 🙁 😰 😕 😣

ENERGY LEVEL AM
1 2 3 4 5 6 7 8 9 10

STRESS LEVEL AM
1 2 3 4 5 6 7 8 9 10

MOOD PM
😄 🙂 😐 🙁 😰 😕 😣

ENERGY LEVEL PM
1 2 3 4 5 6 7 8 9 10

STRESS LEVEL PM
1 2 3 4 5 6 7 8 9 10

TODAY I HAD

	little	enough
water	☐	☐
fruits	☐	☐
vegetables	☐	☐
sleep	☐	☐
fresh air	☐	☐
free time	☐	☐
	☐	☐

👍 POSITIVE EXPERIENCES TODAY

○ success at work   ○ sports activity
○ meeting with friends   ○ good weather
○ time for family   ○ time in nature
○ excursion   ○ delicious food
○ _____   ○ _____

💬 NEGATIVE EXPERIENCES TODAY

○ failure at work   ○ loneliness
○ dispute   ○ bad weather
○ criticism   ○ bad food
○ exclusion   ○ fears
○ _____   ○ _____

WHAT CAN I DO TO MAKE MY NEXT DAY BETTER?

_____

_____

THOUGHTS & REFLECTIONS

_____

_____

_____

_____

DATE: _____   DAY: M T W T F S S

Daily Mood Tracker

TODAY I FEEL

☐ grateful   ☐ motivated   ☐ satisfied   ☐ lonely   ☐ sad   ☐ tired
☐ happy   ☐ productive   ☐ calm   ☐ depressed   ☐ angry   ☐ _____
☐ proud   ☐ relaxed   ☐ powerful   ☐ anxious   ☐ annoyed   ☐ _____

WHY DO I FEEL THIS WAY?

_____

_____

THREE GOALS FOR TODAY

❶ _____

❷ _____

❸ _____

MOOD AM
😄 🙂 😐 🙁 😟 😣 ☹️

ENERGY LEVEL AM
1 2 3 4 5 6 7 8 9 10

STRESS LEVEL AM
1 2 3 4 5 6 7 8 9 10

MOOD PM
😄 🙂 😐 🙁 😟 😣 ☹️

ENERGY LEVEL PM
1 2 3 4 5 6 7 8 9 10

STRESS LEVEL PM
1 2 3 4 5 6 7 8 9 10

TODAY I HAD

	little	enough
water	☐	☐
fruits	☐	☐
vegetables	☐	☐
sleep	☐	☐
fresh air	☐	☐
free time	☐	☐
	☐	☐

👍 POSITIVE EXPERIENCES TODAY

○ success at work   ○ sports activity
○ meeting with friends   ○ good weather
○ time for family   ○ time in nature
○ excursion   ○ delicious food
○ _____   ○ _____

💬 NEGATIVE EXPERIENCES TODAY

○ failure at work   ○ loneliness
○ dispute   ○ bad weather
○ criticism   ○ bad food
○ exclusion   ○ fears
○ _____   ○ _____

WHAT CAN I DO TO MAKE MY NEXT DAY BETTER?

_____

_____

THOUGHTS & REFLECTIONS

_____

_____

_____

_____

Daily *Mood* Tracker

DATE: _____

DAY: M T W T F S S

TODAY I FEEL

☐ grateful   ☐ motivated   ☐ satisfied   ☐ lonely   ☐ sad   ☐ tired
☐ happy   ☐ productive   ☐ calm   ☐ depressed   ☐ angry   ☐ _____
☐ proud   ☐ relaxed   ☐ powerful   ☐ anxious   ☐ annoyed   ☐ _____

WHY DO I FEEL THIS WAY?

_____

_____

THREE GOALS FOR TODAY

1 _____

2 _____

3 _____

MOOD AM

☺ ☺ ☺ ☹ ☹ ☹ ☹

ENERGY LEVEL AM

1 2 3 4 5 6 7 8 9 10

STRESS LEVEL AM

1 2 3 4 5 6 7 8 9 10

MOOD PM

☺ ☺ ☺ ☹ ☹ ☹ ☹

ENERGY LEVEL PM

1 2 3 4 5 6 7 8 9 10

STRESS LEVEL PM

1 2 3 4 5 6 7 8 9 10

TODAY I HAD

	little	enough
water	☐	☐
fruits	☐	☐
vegetables	☐	☐
sleep	☐	☐
fresh air	☐	☐
free time	☐	☐
	☐	☐

👍 POSITIVE EXPERIENCES TODAY

○ success at work   ○ sports activity
○ meeting with friends   ○ good weather
○ time for family   ○ time in nature
○ excursion   ○ delicious food
○ _____   ○ _____

👎 NEGATIVE EXPERIENCES TODAY

○ failure at work   ○ loneliness
○ dispute   ○ bad weather
○ criticism   ○ bad food
○ exclusion   ○ fears
○ _____   ○ _____

WHAT CAN I DO TO MAKE MY NEXT DAY BETTER?

_____

_____

THOUGHTS & REFLECTIONS

_____

_____

_____

_____

DATE: _____   DAY: M T W T F S S

Daily Mood Tracker

TODAY I FEEL

☐ grateful	☐ motivated	☐ satisfied	☐ lonely	☐ sad	☐ tired
☐ happy	☐ productive	☐ calm	☐ depressed	☐ angry	☐ _____
☐ proud	☐ relaxed	☐ powerful	☐ anxious	☐ annoyed	☐ _____

WHY DO I FEEL THIS WAY?

_____

_____

THREE GOALS FOR TODAY

1 _____

2 _____

3 _____

MOOD AM

😄 🙂 😐 🙁 😕 😣 ☹️

ENERGY LEVEL AM

1 2 3 4 5 6 7 8 9 10

STRESS LEVEL AM

1 2 3 4 5 6 7 8 9 10

MOOD PM

😄 🙂 😐 🙁 😕 😣 ☹️

ENERGY LEVEL PM

1 2 3 4 5 6 7 8 9 10

STRESS LEVEL PM

1 2 3 4 5 6 7 8 9 10

TODAY I HAD

	little	enough
water	☐	☐
fruits	☐	☐
vegetables	☐	☐
sleep	☐	☐
fresh air	☐	☐
free time	☐	☐
	☐	☐

👍 POSITIVE EXPERIENCES TODAY

○ success at work	○ sports activity
○ meeting with friends	○ good weather
○ time for family	○ time in nature
○ excursion	○ delicious food
○ _____	○ _____

👎 NEGATIVE EXPERIENCES TODAY

○ failure at work	○ loneliness
○ dispute	○ bad weather
○ criticism	○ bad food
○ exclusion	○ fears
○ _____	○ _____

WHAT CAN I DO TO MAKE MY NEXT DAY BETTER?

_____

_____

THOUGHTS & REFLECTIONS

_____

_____

_____

_____

DATE:_____   DAY: M T W T F S S

Daily *Mood* Tracker

TODAY I FEEL

- ☐ grateful
- ☐ happy
- ☐ proud
- ☐ motivated
- ☐ productive
- ☐ relaxed
- ☐ satisfied
- ☐ calm
- ☐ powerful
- ☐ lonely
- ☐ depressed
- ☐ anxious
- ☐ sad
- ☐ angry
- ☐ annoyed
- ☐ tired
- ☐ _____
- ☐ _____

WHY DO I FEEL THIS WAY?

_____

_____

THREE GOALS FOR TODAY

1 _____

2 _____

3 _____

MOOD AM

☺ ☺ ☺ ☹ ☺ ☹ ☹

ENERGY LEVEL AM

1 2 3 4 5 6 7 8 9 10

STRESS LEVEL AM

1 2 3 4 5 6 7 8 9 10

MOOD PM

☺ ☺ ☺ ☹ ☺ ☹ ☹

ENERGY LEVEL PM

1 2 3 4 5 6 7 8 9 10

STRESS LEVEL PM

1 2 3 4 5 6 7 8 9 10

TODAY I HAD

	little	enough
water	☐	☐
fruits	☐	☐
vegetables	☐	☐
sleep	☐	☐
fresh air	☐	☐
free time	☐	☐
	☐	☐

👍 POSITIVE EXPERIENCES TODAY

- ○ success at work
- ○ meeting with friends
- ○ time for family
- ○ excursion
- ○ _____
- ○ sports activity
- ○ good weather
- ○ time in nature
- ○ delicious food
- ○ _____

👎 NEGATIVE EXPERIENCES TODAY

- ○ failure at work
- ○ dispute
- ○ criticism
- ○ exclusion
- ○ _____
- ○ loneliness
- ○ bad weather
- ○ bad food
- ○ fears
- ○ _____

WHAT CAN I DO TO MAKE MY NEXT DAY BETTER?

_____

_____

THOUGHTS & REFLECTIONS

_____

_____

_____

_____

DATE: _____   DAY: M T W T F S S

Daily Mood Tracker

TODAY I FEEL

☐ grateful ☐ motivated ☐ satisfied ☐ lonely ☐ sad ☐ tired
☐ happy ☐ productive ☐ calm ☐ depressed ☐ angry ☐ _____
☐ proud ☐ relaxed ☐ powerful ☐ anxious ☐ annoyed ☐ _____

WHY DO I FEEL THIS WAY?

_____

_____

THREE GOALS FOR TODAY

1 _____

2 _____

3 _____

MOOD AM

☺ ☺ ☺ ☹ ☹ ☹ ☹

ENERGY LEVEL AM

1 2 3 4 5 6 7 8 9 10

STRESS LEVEL AM

1 2 3 4 5 6 7 8 9 10

MOOD PM

☺ ☺ ☺ ☹ ☹ ☹ ☹

ENERGY LEVEL PM

1 2 3 4 5 6 7 8 9 10

STRESS LEVEL PM

1 2 3 4 5 6 7 8 9 10

TODAY I HAD

	little	enough
water	☐	☐
fruits	☐	☐
vegetables	☐	☐
sleep	☐	☐
fresh air	☐	☐
free time	☐	☐
	☐	☐

👍 POSITIVE EXPERIENCES TODAY

○ success at work   ○ sports activity
○ meeting with friends ○ good weather
○ time for family   ○ time in nature
○ excursion   ○ delicious food
○ _____   ○ _____

💬 NEGATIVE EXPERIENCES TODAY

○ failure at work ○ loneliness
○ dispute   ○ bad weather
○ criticism   ○ bad food
○ exclusion   ○ fears
○ _____ ○ _____

WHAT CAN I DO TO MAKE MY NEXT DAY BETTER?

_____

_____

THOUGHTS & REFLECTIONS

_____

_____

_____

_____

DATE: _____   DAY: M T W T F S S

Daily *Mood* Tracker

TODAY I FEEL

☐ grateful   ☐ motivated   ☐ satisfied   ☐ lonely   ☐ sad   ☐ tired
☐ happy   ☐ productive   ☐ calm   ☐ depressed   ☐ angry   ☐ _____
☐ proud   ☐ relaxed   ☐ powerful   ☐ anxious   ☐ annoyed   ☐ _____

WHY DO I FEEL THIS WAY?

_____

_____

THREE GOALS FOR TODAY

1 _____

2 _____

3 _____

MOOD AM
☺ ☺ ☺ ☹ ☹ ☹ ☹

ENERGY LEVEL AM
1 2 3 4 5 6 7 8 9 10

STRESS LEVEL AM
1 2 3 4 5 6 7 8 9 10

MOOD PM
☺ ☺ ☺ ☹ ☹ ☹ ☹

ENERGY LEVEL PM
1 2 3 4 5 6 7 8 9 10

STRESS LEVEL PM
1 2 3 4 5 6 7 8 9 10

TODAY I HAD

	little	enough
water	☐	☐
fruits	☐	☐
vegetables	☐	☐
sleep	☐	☐
fresh air	☐	☐
free time	☐	☐
	☐	☐

👍 POSITIVE EXPERIENCES TODAY

○ success at work   ○ sports activity
○ meeting with friends   ○ good weather
○ time for family   ○ time in nature
○ excursion   ○ delicious food
○ _____   ○ _____

👎 NEGATIVE EXPERIENCES TODAY

○ failure at work   ○ loneliness
○ dispute   ○ bad weather
○ criticism   ○ bad food
○ exclusion   ○ fears
○ _____   ○ _____

WHAT CAN I DO TO MAKE MY NEXT DAY BETTER?

_____

_____

THOUGHTS & REFLECTIONS

_____

_____

_____

_____

DATE: _____   DAY: M T W T F S S

Daily *Mood* Tracker

TODAY I FEEL

- ☐ grateful
- ☐ happy
- ☐ proud
- ☐ motivated
- ☐ productive
- ☐ relaxed
- ☐ satisfied
- ☐ calm
- ☐ powerful
- ☐ lonely
- ☐ depressed
- ☐ anxious
- ☐ sad
- ☐ angry
- ☐ annoyed
- ☐ tired
- ☐ _____
- ☐ _____

WHY DO I FEEL THIS WAY?

_____

_____

THREE GOALS FOR TODAY

1 _____

2 _____

3 _____

MOOD AM

☺ ☺ ☺ ☹ ☹ ☹ ☹

ENERGY LEVEL AM

1 2 3 4 5 6 7 8 9 10

STRESS LEVEL AM

1 2 3 4 5 6 7 8 9 10

MOOD PM

☺ ☺ ☺ ☹ ☹ ☹ ☹

ENERGY LEVEL PM

1 2 3 4 5 6 7 8 9 10

STRESS LEVEL PM

1 2 3 4 5 6 7 8 9 10

TODAY I HAD

	little	enough
water	☐	☐
fruits	☐	☐
vegetables	☐	☐
sleep	☐	☐
fresh air	☐	☐
free time	☐	☐
	☐	☐

👍 POSITIVE EXPERIENCES TODAY

- ○ success at work
- ○ meeting with friends
- ○ time for family
- ○ excursion
- ○ _____
- ○ sports activity
- ○ good weather
- ○ time in nature
- ○ delicious food
- ○ _____

💬 NEGATIVE EXPERIENCES TODAY

- ○ failure at work
- ○ dispute
- ○ criticism
- ○ exclusion
- ○ _____
- ○ loneliness
- ○ bad weather
- ○ bad food
- ○ fears
- ○ _____

WHAT CAN I DO TO MAKE MY NEXT DAY BETTER?

_____

_____

THOUGHTS & REFLECTIONS

_____

_____

_____

_____

DATE: _____   # Daily *Mood* Tracker   DAY: M T W T F S S

TODAY I FEEL

☐ grateful   ☐ motivated   ☐ satisfied   ☐ lonely   ☐ sad   ☐ tired
☐ happy   ☐ productive   ☐ calm   ☐ depressed   ☐ angry   ☐ _____
☐ proud   ☐ relaxed   ☐ powerful   ☐ anxious   ☐ annoyed   ☐ _____

WHY DO I FEEL THIS WAY?

_____

_____

THREE GOALS FOR TODAY

1 _____

2 _____

3 _____

MOOD AM

☺ ☺ ☺ ☹ ☹ ☹ ☹

ENERGY LEVEL AM

1 2 3 4 5 6 7 8 9 10

STRESS LEVEL AM

1 2 3 4 5 6 7 8 9 10

MOOD PM

☺ ☺ ☺ ☹ ☹ ☹ ☹

ENERGY LEVEL PM

1 2 3 4 5 6 7 8 9 10

STRESS LEVEL PM

1 2 3 4 5 6 7 8 9 10

TODAY I HAD

	little	enough
water	☐	☐
fruits	☐	☐
vegetables	☐	☐
sleep	☐	☐
fresh air	☐	☐
free time	☐	☐
	☐	☐

👍 POSITIVE EXPERIENCES TODAY

○ success at work   ○ sports activity
○ meeting with friends   ○ good weather
○ time for family   ○ time in nature
○ excursion   ○ delicious food
○ _____   ○ _____

👎 NEGATIVE EXPERIENCES TODAY

○ failure at work   ○ loneliness
○ dispute   ○ bad weather
○ criticism   ○ bad food
○ exclusion   ○ fears
○ _____   ○ _____

WHAT CAN I DO TO MAKE MY NEXT DAY BETTER?

_____

_____

THOUGHTS & REFLECTIONS

_____

_____

_____

_____

DATE: _____   DAY: M T W T F S S

Daily Mood Tracker

TODAY I FEEL

- ☐ grateful
- ☐ happy
- ☐ proud
- ☐ motivated
- ☐ productive
- ☐ relaxed
- ☐ satisfied
- ☐ calm
- ☐ powerful
- ☐ lonely
- ☐ depressed
- ☐ anxious
- ☐ sad
- ☐ angry
- ☐ annoyed
- ☐ tired
- ☐ _____
- ☐ _____

WHY DO I FEEL THIS WAY?

_____

_____

THREE GOALS FOR TODAY

❶ _____

❷ _____

❸ _____

MOOD AM

☺ ☺ ☺ ☹ ☹ ☹ ☹

ENERGY LEVEL AM

1 2 3 4 5 6 7 8 9 10

STRESS LEVEL AM

1 2 3 4 5 6 7 8 9 10

MOOD PM

☺ ☺ ☺ ☹ ☹ ☹ ☹

ENERGY LEVEL PM

1 2 3 4 5 6 7 8 9 10

STRESS LEVEL PM

1 2 3 4 5 6 7 8 9 10

TODAY I HAD

	little	enough
water	☐	☐
fruits	☐	☐
vegetables	☐	☐
sleep	☐	☐
fresh air	☐	☐
free time	☐	☐
	☐	☐

👍 POSITIVE EXPERIENCES TODAY

- ○ success at work
- ○ meeting with friends
- ○ time for family
- ○ excursion
- ○ _____
- ○ sports activity
- ○ good weather
- ○ time in nature
- ○ delicious food
- ○ _____

👎 NEGATIVE EXPERIENCES TODAY

- ○ failure at work
- ○ dispute
- ○ criticism
- ○ exclusion
- ○ _____
- ○ loneliness
- ○ bad weather
- ○ bad food
- ○ fears
- ○ _____

WHAT CAN I DO TO MAKE MY NEXT DAY BETTER?

_____

_____

THOUGHTS & REFLECTIONS

_____

_____

_____

_____

DATE: _____ DAY: M T W T F S S

Daily *Mood* Tracker

TODAY I FEEL

☐ grateful ☐ motivated ☐ satisfied ☐ lonely ☐ sad ☐ tired
☐ happy ☐ productive ☐ calm ☐ depressed ☐ angry ☐ _____
☐ proud ☐ relaxed ☐ powerful ☐ anxious ☐ annoyed ☐ _____

WHY DO I FEEL THIS WAY?

_____

_____

THREE GOALS FOR TODAY

1 _____

2 _____

3 _____

MOOD AM

☺ ☺ ☺ ☹ ☹ ☹ ☹

ENERGY LEVEL AM

1 2 3 4 5 6 7 8 9 10

STRESS LEVEL AM

1 2 3 4 5 6 7 8 9 10

MOOD PM

☺ ☺ ☺ ☹ ☹ ☹ ☹

ENERGY LEVEL PM

1 2 3 4 5 6 7 8 9 10

STRESS LEVEL PM

1 2 3 4 5 6 7 8 9 10

TODAY I HAD

	little	enough
water	☐	☐
fruits	☐	☐
vegetables	☐	☐
sleep	☐	☐
fresh air	☐	☐
free time	☐	☐
	☐	☐

👍 POSITIVE EXPERIENCES TODAY

○ success at work ○ sports activity
○ meeting with friends ○ good weather
○ time for family ○ time in nature
○ excursion ○ delicious food
○ _____ ○ _____

💬 NEGATIVE EXPERIENCES TODAY

○ failure at work ○ loneliness
○ dispute ○ bad weather
○ criticism ○ bad food
○ exclusion ○ fears
○ _____ ○ _____

WHAT CAN I DO TO MAKE MY NEXT DAY BETTER?

_____

_____

THOUGHTS & REFLECTIONS

_____

_____

_____

_____

DATE: _____   DAY: M T W T F S S

Daily *Mood* Tracker

TODAY I FEEL

☐ grateful   ☐ motivated   ☐ satisfied   ☐ lonely   ☐ sad   ☐ tired
☐ happy   ☐ productive   ☐ calm   ☐ depressed   ☐ angry   ☐ _____
☐ proud   ☐ relaxed   ☐ powerful   ☐ anxious   ☐ annoyed   ☐ _____

WHY DO I FEEL THIS WAY?

_____

_____

THREE GOALS FOR TODAY

1 _____

2 _____

3 _____

MOOD AM

😀 🙂 😐 🙁 😣 😫 ☹️

ENERGY LEVEL AM

1 2 3 4 5 6 7 8 9 10

STRESS LEVEL AM

1 2 3 4 5 6 7 8 9 10

MOOD PM

😀 🙂 😐 🙁 😣 😫 ☹️

ENERGY LEVEL PM

1 2 3 4 5 6 7 8 9 10

STRESS LEVEL PM

1 2 3 4 5 6 7 8 9 10

TODAY I HAD

	little	enough
water	☐	☐
fruits	☐	☐
vegetables	☐	☐
sleep	☐	☐
fresh air	☐	☐
free time	☐	☐
	☐	☐

👍 POSITIVE EXPERIENCES TODAY

○ success at work   ○ sports activity
○ meeting with friends   ○ good weather
○ time for family   ○ time in nature
○ excursion   ○ delicious food
○ _____   ○ _____

👎 NEGATIVE EXPERIENCES TODAY

○ failure at work   ○ loneliness
○ dispute   ○ bad weather
○ criticism   ○ bad food
○ exclusion   ○ fears
○ _____   ○ _____

WHAT CAN I DO TO MAKE MY NEXT DAY BETTER?

_____

_____

THOUGHTS & REFLECTIONS

_____

_____

_____

_____

DATE:_____   DAY: M T W T F S S

Daily *Mood* Tracker

TODAY I FEEL

☐ grateful   ☐ motivated   ☐ satisfied   ☐ lonely   ☐ sad   ☐ tired
☐ happy   ☐ productive   ☐ calm   ☐ depressed   ☐ angry   ☐ _____
☐ proud   ☐ relaxed   ☐ powerful   ☐ anxious   ☐ annoyed   ☐ _____

WHY DO I FEEL THIS WAY?

_____

_____

THREE GOALS FOR TODAY

1 _____

2 _____

3 _____

MOOD AM

☺ ☺ ☺ ☹ ☹ ☹ ☹

ENERGY LEVEL AM

1 2 3 4 5 6 7 8 9 10

STRESS LEVEL AM

1 2 3 4 5 6 7 8 9 10

MOOD PM

☺ ☺ ☺ ☹ ☹ ☹ ☹

ENERGY LEVEL PM

1 2 3 4 5 6 7 8 9 10

STRESS LEVEL PM

1 2 3 4 5 6 7 8 9 10

TODAY I HAD

	little	enough
water	☐	☐
fruits	☐	☐
vegetables	☐	☐
sleep	☐	☐
fresh air	☐	☐
free time	☐	☐
	☐	☐

👍 POSITIVE EXPERIENCES TODAY

○ success at work   ○ sports activity
○ meeting with friends ○ good weather
○ time for family   ○ time in nature
○ excursion   ○ delicious food
○ _____   ○ _____

💬 NEGATIVE EXPERIENCES TODAY

○ failure at work   ○ loneliness
○ dispute   ○ bad weather
○ criticism   ○ bad food
○ exclusion   ○ fears
○ _____   ○ _____

WHAT CAN I DO TO MAKE MY NEXT DAY BETTER?

_____

_____

THOUGHTS & REFLECTIONS

_____

_____

_____

_____

DATE: _____

Daily *Mood* Tracker

DAY: M T W T F S S

TODAY I FEEL

- ☐ grateful
- ☐ happy
- ☐ proud
- ☐ motivated
- ☐ productive
- ☐ relaxed
- ☐ satisfied
- ☐ calm
- ☐ powerful
- ☐ lonely
- ☐ depressed
- ☐ anxious
- ☐ sad
- ☐ angry
- ☐ annoyed
- ☐ tired
- ☐ _____
- ☐ _____

WHY DO I FEEL THIS WAY?

_____

_____

THREE GOALS FOR TODAY

1 _____

2 _____

3 _____

MOOD AM

😃 🙂 😐 🙁 😟 😖 ☹️

ENERGY LEVEL AM

1 2 3 4 5 6 7 8 9 10

STRESS LEVEL AM

1 2 3 4 5 6 7 8 9 10

MOOD PM

😃 🙂 😐 🙁 😟 😖 ☹️

ENERGY LEVEL PM

1 2 3 4 5 6 7 8 9 10

STRESS LEVEL PM

1 2 3 4 5 6 7 8 9 10

TODAY I HAD

	little	enough
water	☐	☐
fruits	☐	☐
vegetables	☐	☐
sleep	☐	☐
fresh air	☐	☐
free time	☐	☐
	☐	☐

👍 POSITIVE EXPERIENCES TODAY

- ○ success at work
- ○ meeting with friends
- ○ time for family
- ○ excursion
- ○ _____
- ○ sports activity
- ○ good weather
- ○ time in nature
- ○ delicious food
- ○ _____

💬 NEGATIVE EXPERIENCES TODAY

- ○ failure at work
- ○ dispute
- ○ criticism
- ○ exclusion
- ○ _____
- ○ loneliness
- ○ bad weather
- ○ bad food
- ○ fears
- ○ _____

WHAT CAN I DO TO MAKE MY NEXT DAY BETTER?

_____

_____

THOUGHTS & REFLECTIONS

_____

_____

_____

_____

DATE: _____   DAY: M T W T F S S

Daily *Mood* Tracker

TODAY I FEEL

- ☐ grateful
- ☐ happy
- ☐ proud
- ☐ motivated
- ☐ productive
- ☐ relaxed
- ☐ satisfied
- ☐ calm
- ☐ powerful
- ☐ lonely
- ☐ depressed
- ☐ anxious
- ☐ sad
- ☐ angry
- ☐ annoyed
- ☐ tired
- ☐ _____
- ☐ _____

WHY DO I FEEL THIS WAY?

_____

_____

THREE GOALS FOR TODAY

1 _____

2 _____

3 _____

MOOD AM

☺ ☺ ☺ ☹ ☹ ☹ ☹

ENERGY LEVEL AM

1 2 3 4 5 6 7 8 9 10

STRESS LEVEL AM

1 2 3 4 5 6 7 8 9 10

MOOD PM

☺ ☺ ☺ ☹ ☹ ☹ ☹

ENERGY LEVEL PM

1 2 3 4 5 6 7 8 9 10

STRESS LEVEL PM

1 2 3 4 5 6 7 8 9 10

TODAY I HAD

	little	enough
water	☐	☐
fruits	☐	☐
vegetables	☐	☐
sleep	☐	☐
fresh air	☐	☐
free time	☐	☐
	☐	☐

👍 POSITIVE EXPERIENCES TODAY

- ○ success at work
- ○ meeting with friends
- ○ time for family
- ○ excursion
- ○ _____
- ○ sports activity
- ○ good weather
- ○ time in nature
- ○ delicious food
- ○ _____

💬 NEGATIVE EXPERIENCES TODAY

- ○ failure at work
- ○ dispute
- ○ criticism
- ○ exclusion
- ○ _____
- ○ loneliness
- ○ bad weather
- ○ bad food
- ○ fears
- ○ _____

WHAT CAN I DO TO MAKE MY NEXT DAY BETTER?

_____

_____

THOUGHTS & REFLECTIONS

_____

_____

_____

_____

DATE: _____

Daily *Mood* Tracker

DAY: M T W T F S S

TODAY I FEEL

☐ grateful   ☐ motivated   ☐ satisfied   ☐ lonely   ☐ sad   ☐ tired
☐ happy   ☐ productive   ☐ calm   ☐ depressed   ☐ angry   ☐ _____
☐ proud   ☐ relaxed   ☐ powerful   ☐ anxious   ☐ annoyed   ☐ _____

WHY DO I FEEL THIS WAY?

_____

_____

THREE GOALS FOR TODAY

❶ _____

❷ _____

❸ _____

MOOD AM

😁 🙂 😐 🙁 😟 😣 😖

ENERGY LEVEL AM

1 2 3 4 5 6 7 8 9 10

STRESS LEVEL AM

1 2 3 4 5 6 7 8 9 10

MOOD PM

😁 🙂 😐 🙁 😟 😣 😖

ENERGY LEVEL PM

1 2 3 4 5 6 7 8 9 10

STRESS LEVEL PM

1 2 3 4 5 6 7 8 9 10

TODAY I HAD

	little	enough
water	☐	☐
fruits	☐	☐
vegetables	☐	☐
sleep	☐	☐
fresh air	☐	☐
free time	☐	☐
	☐	☐

👍 POSITIVE EXPERIENCES TODAY

○ success at work   ○ sports activity
○ meeting with friends ○ good weather
○ time for family   ○ time in nature
○ excursion   ○ delicious food
○ _____   ○ _____

👎 NEGATIVE EXPERIENCES TODAY

○ failure at work   ○ loneliness
○ dispute   ○ bad weather
○ criticism   ○ bad food
○ exclusion   ○ fears
○ _____   ○ _____

WHAT CAN I DO TO MAKE MY NEXT DAY BETTER?

_____

_____

THOUGHTS & REFLECTIONS

_____

_____

_____

_____

DATE: _____

Daily *Mood* Tracker

DAY: M T W T F S S

TODAY I FEEL

☐ grateful   ☐ motivated   ☐ satisfied   ☐ lonely   ☐ sad   ☐ tired
☐ happy   ☐ productive   ☐ calm   ☐ depressed   ☐ angry   ☐ _____
☐ proud   ☐ relaxed   ☐ powerful   ☐ anxious   ☐ annoyed   ☐ _____

WHY DO I FEEL THIS WAY?

_____

_____

THREE GOALS FOR TODAY

1 _____

2 _____

3 _____

MOOD AM

😁 🙂 😐 🙁 😟 😕 😣

ENERGY LEVEL AM

1 2 3 4 5 6 7 8 9 10

STRESS LEVEL AM

1 2 3 4 5 6 7 8 9 10

MOOD PM

😁 🙂 😐 🙁 😟 😕 😣

ENERGY LEVEL PM

1 2 3 4 5 6 7 8 9 10

STRESS LEVEL PM

1 2 3 4 5 6 7 8 9 10

TODAY I HAD

	little	enough
water	☐	☐
fruits	☐	☐
vegetables	☐	☐
sleep	☐	☐
fresh air	☐	☐
free time	☐	☐
	☐	☐

👍 POSITIVE EXPERIENCES TODAY

○ success at work   ○ sports activity
○ meeting with friends   ○ good weather
○ time for family   ○ time in nature
○ excursion   ○ delicious food
○ _____   ○ _____

💬 NEGATIVE EXPERIENCES TODAY

○ failure at work   ○ loneliness
○ dispute   ○ bad weather
○ criticism   ○ bad food
○ exclusion   ○ fears
○ _____   ○ _____

WHAT CAN I DO TO MAKE MY NEXT DAY BETTER?

_____

_____

THOUGHTS & REFLECTIONS

_____

_____

_____

_____

DATE: _____   DAY: M T W T F S S

Daily *Mood* Tracker

TODAY I FEEL

☐ grateful   ☐ motivated   ☐ satisfied   ☐ lonely   ☐ sad   ☐ tired
☐ happy   ☐ productive   ☐ calm   ☐ depressed   ☐ angry   ☐ _____
☐ proud   ☐ relaxed   ☐ powerful   ☐ anxious   ☐ annoyed   ☐ _____

WHY DO I FEEL THIS WAY?

_____

_____

THREE GOALS FOR TODAY

1 _____

2 _____

3 _____

MOOD AM

😀 🙂 😐 🙁 😣 😖 😞

ENERGY LEVEL AM

1 2 3 4 5 6 7 8 9 10

STRESS LEVEL AM

1 2 3 4 5 6 7 8 9 10

MOOD PM

😀 🙂 😐 🙁 😣 😖 😞

ENERGY LEVEL PM

1 2 3 4 5 6 7 8 9 10

STRESS LEVEL PM

1 2 3 4 5 6 7 8 9 10

TODAY I HAD

	little	enough
water	☐	☐
fruits	☐	☐
vegetables	☐	☐
sleep	☐	☐
fresh air	☐	☐
free time	☐	☐
	☐	☐

👍 POSITIVE EXPERIENCES TODAY

○ success at work   ○ sports activity
○ meeting with friends   ○ good weather
○ time for family   ○ time in nature
○ excursion   ○ delicious food
○ _____   ○ _____

👎 NEGATIVE EXPERIENCES TODAY

○ failure at work   ○ loneliness
○ dispute   ○ bad weather
○ criticism   ○ bad food
○ exclusion   ○ fears
○ _____   ○ _____

WHAT CAN I DO TO MAKE MY NEXT DAY BETTER?

_____

_____

THOUGHTS & REFLECTIONS

_____

_____

_____

_____

DATE: _____   DAY: M T W T F S S

Daily *Mood* Tracker

TODAY I FEEL

☐ grateful   ☐ motivated   ☐ satisfied   ☐ lonely   ☐ sad   ☐ tired
☐ happy   ☐ productive   ☐ calm   ☐ depressed   ☐ angry   ☐ _____
☐ proud   ☐ relaxed   ☐ powerful   ☐ anxious   ☐ annoyed   ☐ _____

WHY DO I FEEL THIS WAY?

_____

_____

THREE GOALS FOR TODAY

1 _____

2 _____

3 _____

MOOD AM

☺ ☺ ☺ ☹ ☹ ☹ ☹

ENERGY LEVEL AM

1 2 3 4 5 6 7 8 9 10

STRESS LEVEL AM

1 2 3 4 5 6 7 8 9 10

MOOD PM

☺ ☺ ☺ ☹ ☹ ☹ ☹

ENERGY LEVEL PM

1 2 3 4 5 6 7 8 9 10

STRESS LEVEL PM

1 2 3 4 5 6 7 8 9 10

TODAY I HAD

	little	enough
water	☐	☐
fruits	☐	☐
vegetables	☐	☐
sleep	☐	☐
fresh air	☐	☐
free time	☐	☐
	☐	☐

👍 POSITIVE EXPERIENCES TODAY

○ success at work   ○ sports activity
○ meeting with friends ○ good weather
○ time for family   ○ time in nature
○ excursion   ○ delicious food
○ _____   ○ _____

💬 NEGATIVE EXPERIENCES TODAY

○ failure at work   ○ loneliness
○ dispute   ○ bad weather
○ criticism   ○ bad food
○ exclusion   ○ fears
○ _____   ○ _____

WHAT CAN I DO TO MAKE MY NEXT DAY BETTER?

_____

_____

THOUGHTS & REFLECTIONS

_____

_____

_____

_____

DATE: _____

Daily *Mood* Tracker

DAY: M T W T F S S

TODAY I FEEL

☐ grateful   ☐ motivated   ☐ satisfied   ☐ lonely   ☐ sad   ☐ tired
☐ happy   ☐ productive   ☐ calm   ☐ depressed ☐ angry ☐ _____
☐ proud   ☐ relaxed   ☐ powerful   ☐ anxious   ☐ annoyed ☐ _____

WHY DO I FEEL THIS WAY?

_____

_____

THREE GOALS FOR TODAY

1 _____

2 _____

3 _____

MOOD AM

😄 🙂 😐 😕 🥴 😟 ☹️

ENERGY LEVEL AM

1 2 3 4 5 6 7 8 9 10

STRESS LEVEL AM

1 2 3 4 5 6 7 8 9 10

MOOD PM

😄 🙂 😐 😕 🥴 😟 ☹️

ENERGY LEVEL PM

1 2 3 4 5 6 7 8 9 10

STRESS LEVEL PM

1 2 3 4 5 6 7 8 9 10

TODAY I HAD

	little	enough
water	☐	☐
fruits	☐	☐
vegetables	☐	☐
sleep	☐	☐
fresh air	☐	☐
free time	☐	☐
	☐	☐

👍 POSITIVE EXPERIENCES TODAY

○ success at work   ○ sports activity
○ meeting with friends ○ good weather
○ time for family   ○ time in nature
○ excursion   ○ delicious food
○ _____   ○ _____

💬 NEGATIVE EXPERIENCES TODAY

○ failure at work ○ loneliness
○ dispute   ○ bad weather
○ criticism   ○ bad food
○ exclusion   ○ fears
○ _____   ○ _____

WHAT CAN I DO TO MAKE MY NEXT DAY BETTER?

_____

_____

THOUGHTS & REFLECTIONS

_____

_____

_____

_____

DATE: _____   DAY: M T W T F S S

Daily *Mood* Tracker

TODAY I FEEL

☐ grateful   ☐ motivated   ☐ satisfied   ☐ lonely   ☐ sad   ☐ tired
☐ happy   ☐ productive   ☐ calm   ☐ depressed   ☐ angry   ☐ _____
☐ proud   ☐ relaxed   ☐ powerful   ☐ anxious   ☐ annoyed   ☐ _____

WHY DO I FEEL THIS WAY?

_____

_____

THREE GOALS FOR TODAY

1 _____

2 _____

3 _____

MOOD AM

😃 😊 😐 😟 😵 😖 😣

ENERGY LEVEL AM

1 2 3 4 5 6 7 8 9 10

STRESS LEVEL AM

1 2 3 4 5 6 7 8 9 10

MOOD PM

😃 😊 😐 😟 😵 😖 😣

ENERGY LEVEL PM

1 2 3 4 5 6 7 8 9 10

STRESS LEVEL PM

1 2 3 4 5 6 7 8 9 10

TODAY I HAD

	little	enough
water	☐	☐
fruits	☐	☐
vegetables	☐	☐
sleep	☐	☐
fresh air	☐	☐
free time	☐	☐
	☐	☐

👍 POSITIVE EXPERIENCES TODAY

○ success at work   ○ sports activity
○ meeting with friends   ○ good weather
○ time for family   ○ time in nature
○ excursion   ○ delicious food
○ _____   ○ _____

👎 NEGATIVE EXPERIENCES TODAY

○ failure at work   ○ loneliness
○ dispute   ○ bad weather
○ criticism   ○ bad food
○ exclusion   ○ fears
○ _____   ○ _____

WHAT CAN I DO TO MAKE MY NEXT DAY BETTER?

_____

_____

THOUGHTS & REFLECTIONS

_____

_____

_____

_____

DATE: _____

Daily Mood Tracker

TODAY I FEEL

- ☐ grateful
- ☐ happy
- ☐ proud

- ☐ motivated
- ☐ productive
- ☐ relaxed

- ☐ satisfied
- ☐ calm
- ☐ powerful

- ☐ lonely
- ☐ depressed
- ☐ anxious

- ☐ sad
- ☐ angry
- ☐ annoyed

- ☐ tired
- ☐ _____
- ☐ _____

WHY DO I FEEL THIS WAY?

_____

_____

THREE GOALS FOR TODAY

1 _____

2 _____

3 _____

MOOD AM

😄 🙂 😐 🙁 😟 😕 ☹️

ENERGY LEVEL AM

1 2 3 4 5 6 7 8 9 10

STRESS LEVEL AM

1 2 3 4 5 6 7 8 9 10

MOOD PM

😄 🙂 😐 🙁 😟 😕 ☹️

ENERGY LEVEL PM

1 2 3 4 5 6 7 8 9 10

STRESS LEVEL PM

1 2 3 4 5 6 7 8 9 10

TODAY I HAD

	little	enough
water	☐	☐
fruits	☐	☐
vegetables	☐	☐
sleep	☐	☐
fresh air	☐	☐
free time	☐	☐
	☐	☐

👍 POSITIVE EXPERIENCES TODAY

- ○ success at work
- ○ meeting with friends
- ○ time for family
- ○ excursion
- ○ _____

- ○ sports activity
- ○ good weather
- ○ time in nature
- ○ delicious food
- ○ _____

👎 NEGATIVE EXPERIENCES TODAY

- ○ failure at work
- ○ dispute
- ○ criticism
- ○ exclusion
- ○ _____

- ○ loneliness
- ○ bad weather
- ○ bad food
- ○ fears
- ○ _____

WHAT CAN I DO TO MAKE MY NEXT DAY BETTER?

_____

_____

THOUGHTS & REFLECTIONS

_____

_____

_____

_____

DATE: _____

Daily *Mood* Tracker

TODAY I FEEL

☐ grateful   ☐ motivated   ☐ satisfied   ☐ lonely   ☐ sad   ☐ tired
☐ happy   ☐ productive   ☐ calm   ☐ depressed   ☐ angry   ☐ _____
☐ proud   ☐ relaxed   ☐ powerful   ☐ anxious   ☐ annoyed   ☐ _____

WHY DO I FEEL THIS WAY?

_____

_____

THREE GOALS FOR TODAY

❶ _____

❷ _____

❸ _____

MOOD AM
😄 🙂 😐 🙁 😕 😣 ☹️

ENERGY LEVEL AM
1 2 3 4 5 6 7 8 9 10

STRESS LEVEL AM
1 2 3 4 5 6 7 8 9 10

MOOD PM
😄 🙂 😐 🙁 😕 😣 ☹️

ENERGY LEVEL PM
1 2 3 4 5 6 7 8 9 10

STRESS LEVEL PM
1 2 3 4 5 6 7 8 9 10

TODAY I HAD

	little	enough
water	☐	☐
fruits	☐	☐
vegetables	☐	☐
sleep	☐	☐
fresh air	☐	☐
free time	☐	☐
	☐	☐

👍 POSITIVE EXPERIENCES TODAY

○ success at work   ○ sports activity
○ meeting with friends   ○ good weather
○ time for family   ○ time in nature
○ excursion   ○ delicious food
○ _____   ○ _____

👎 NEGATIVE EXPERIENCES TODAY

○ failure at work   ○ loneliness
○ dispute   ○ bad weather
○ criticism   ○ bad food
○ exclusion   ○ fears
○ _____   ○ _____

WHAT CAN I DO TO MAKE MY NEXT DAY BETTER?

_____

_____

THOUGHTS & REFLECTIONS

_____

_____

_____

_____

DATE: _____

Daily *Mood* Tracker

DAY: M T W T F S S

TODAY I FEEL

- ☐ grateful
- ☐ happy
- ☐ proud

- ☐ motivated
- ☐ productive
- ☐ relaxed

- ☐ satisfied
- ☐ calm
- ☐ powerful

- ☐ lonely
- ☐ depressed
- ☐ anxious

- ☐ sad
- ☐ angry
- ☐ annoyed

- ☐ tired
- ☐ _____
- ☐ _____

WHY DO I FEEL THIS WAY?

_____

_____

THREE GOALS FOR TODAY

1 _____

2 _____

3 _____

MOOD AM

☺ ☺ 😐 😕 😟 😖 😣

ENERGY LEVEL AM

1 2 3 4 5 6 7 8 9 10

STRESS LEVEL AM

1 2 3 4 5 6 7 8 9 10

MOOD PM

☺ ☺ 😐 😕 😟 😖 😣

ENERGY LEVEL PM

1 2 3 4 5 6 7 8 9 10

STRESS LEVEL PM

1 2 3 4 5 6 7 8 9 10

TODAY I HAD

	little	enough
water	☐	☐
fruits	☐	☐
vegetables	☐	☐
sleep	☐	☐
fresh air	☐	☐
free time	☐	☐
	☐	☐

👍 POSITIVE EXPERIENCES TODAY

- ○ success at work
- ○ meeting with friends
- ○ time for family
- ○ excursion
- ○ _____

- ○ sports activity
- ○ good weather
- ○ time in nature
- ○ delicious food
- ○ _____

👎 NEGATIVE EXPERIENCES TODAY

- ○ failure at work
- ○ dispute
- ○ criticism
- ○ exclusion
- ○ _____

- ○ loneliness
- ○ bad weather
- ○ bad food
- ○ fears
- ○ _____

WHAT CAN I DO TO MAKE MY NEXT DAY BETTER?

_____

_____

THOUGHTS & REFLECTIONS

_____

_____

_____

DATE: _____   DAY: M T W T F S S

Daily *Mood* Tracker

TODAY I FEEL

☐ grateful   ☐ motivated   ☐ satisfied   ☐ lonely   ☐ sad   ☐ tired
☐ happy   ☐ productive   ☐ calm   ☐ depressed   ☐ angry   ☐ _____
☐ proud   ☐ relaxed   ☐ powerful   ☐ anxious   ☐ annoyed   ☐ _____

WHY DO I FEEL THIS WAY?

_____

_____

THREE GOALS FOR TODAY

1 _____

2 _____

3 _____

MOOD AM

☺ ☺ ☺ ☺ ☺ ☺ ☺

ENERGY LEVEL AM

1 2 3 4 5 6 7 8 9 10

STRESS LEVEL AM

1 2 3 4 5 6 7 8 9 10

MOOD PM

☺ ☺ ☺ ☺ ☺ ☺ ☺

ENERGY LEVEL PM

1 2 3 4 5 6 7 8 9 10

STRESS LEVEL PM

1 2 3 4 5 6 7 8 9 10

TODAY I HAD

	little	enough
water	☐	☐
fruits	☐	☐
vegetables	☐	☐
sleep	☐	☐
fresh air	☐	☐
free time	☐	☐
	☐	☐

👍 POSITIVE EXPERIENCES TODAY

○ success at work   ○ sports activity
○ meeting with friends   ○ good weather
○ time for family   ○ time in nature
○ excursion   ○ delicious food
○ _____   ○ _____

💬 NEGATIVE EXPERIENCES TODAY

○ failure at work   ○ loneliness
○ dispute   ○ bad weather
○ criticism   ○ bad food
○ exclusion   ○ fears
○ _____   ○ _____

WHAT CAN I DO TO MAKE MY NEXT DAY BETTER?

_____

_____

THOUGHTS & REFLECTIONS

_____

_____

_____

_____

DATE:_____ Daily *Mood* Tracker   DAY: M T W T F S S

TODAY I FEEL

- ☐ grateful
- ☐ happy
- ☐ proud
- ☐ motivated
- ☐ productive
- ☐ relaxed
- ☐ satisfied
- ☐ calm
- ☐ powerful
- ☐ lonely
- ☐ depressed
- ☐ anxious
- ☐ sad
- ☐ angry
- ☐ annoyed
- ☐ tired
- ☐ _____
- ☐ _____

WHY DO I FEEL THIS WAY?

_____
_____

THREE GOALS FOR TODAY

1 _____

2 _____

3 _____

MOOD AM

😃 🙂 😐 🙁 😥 😖 😣

ENERGY LEVEL AM

1 2 3 4 5 6 7 8 9 10

STRESS LEVEL AM

1 2 3 4 5 6 7 8 9 10

MOOD PM

😃 🙂 😐 🙁 😥 😖 😣

ENERGY LEVEL PM

1 2 3 4 5 6 7 8 9 10

STRESS LEVEL PM

1 2 3 4 5 6 7 8 9 10

TODAY I HAD

	little	enough
water	☐	☐
fruits	☐	☐
vegetables	☐	☐
sleep	☐	☐
fresh air	☐	☐
free time	☐	☐
	☐	☐

👍 POSITIVE EXPERIENCES TODAY

- ○ success at work
- ○ meeting with friends
- ○ time for family
- ○ excursion
- ○ _____
- ○ sports activity
- ○ good weather
- ○ time in nature
- ○ delicious food
- ○ _____

💬 NEGATIVE EXPERIENCES TODAY

- ○ failure at work
- ○ dispute
- ○ criticism
- ○ exclusion
- ○ _____
- ○ loneliness
- ○ bad weather
- ○ bad food
- ○ fears
- ○ _____

WHAT CAN I DO TO MAKE MY NEXT DAY BETTER?

_____
_____
_____

THOUGHTS & REFLECTIONS

_____
_____
_____
_____

DATE: _____   DAY: M T W T F S S

Daily Mood Tracker

TODAY I FEEL

☐ grateful   ☐ motivated   ☐ satisfied   ☐ lonely   ☐ sad   ☐ tired
☐ happy   ☐ productive   ☐ calm   ☐ depressed   ☐ angry   ☐ _____
☐ proud   ☐ relaxed   ☐ powerful   ☐ anxious   ☐ annoyed   ☐ _____

WHY DO I FEEL THIS WAY?

_____

_____

THREE GOALS FOR TODAY

1 _____

2 _____

3 _____

MOOD AM

😃 🙂 😐 🙁 😣 😟 😖

ENERGY LEVEL AM

1 2 3 4 5 6 7 8 9 10

STRESS LEVEL AM

1 2 3 4 5 6 7 8 9 10

MOOD PM

😃 🙂 😐 🙁 😣 😟 😖

ENERGY LEVEL PM

1 2 3 4 5 6 7 8 9 10

STRESS LEVEL PM

1 2 3 4 5 6 7 8 9 10

TODAY I HAD

	little	enough
water	☐	☐
fruits	☐	☐
vegetables	☐	☐
sleep	☐	☐
fresh air	☐	☐
free time	☐	☐
	☐	☐

👍 POSITIVE EXPERIENCES TODAY

○ success at work   ○ sports activity
○ meeting with friends ○ good weather
○ time for family   ○ time in nature
○ excursion   ○ delicious food
○ _____   ○ _____

👎 NEGATIVE EXPERIENCES TODAY

○ failure at work   ○ loneliness
○ dispute   ○ bad weather
○ criticism   ○ bad food
○ exclusion   ○ fears
○ _____   ○ _____

WHAT CAN I DO TO MAKE MY NEXT DAY BETTER?

_____

_____

THOUGHTS & REFLECTIONS

_____

_____

_____

_____

DATE: _____   DAY: M T W T F S S

Daily *Mood* Tracker

TODAY I FEEL

☐ grateful   ☐ motivated   ☐ satisfied   ☐ lonely   ☐ sad   ☐ tired
☐ happy   ☐ productive   ☐ calm   ☐ depressed ☐ angry   ☐ _____
☐ proud   ☐ relaxed   ☐ powerful   ☐ anxious   ☐ annoyed   ☐ _____

WHY DO I FEEL THIS WAY?

_____

_____

THREE GOALS FOR TODAY

1 _____

2 _____

3 _____

MOOD AM

😄 🙂 😐 🙁 😕 😖 ☹️

ENERGY LEVEL AM

1 2 3 4 5 6 7 8 9 10

STRESS LEVEL AM

1 2 3 4 5 6 7 8 9 10

MOOD PM

😄 🙂 😐 🙁 😕 😖 ☹️

ENERGY LEVEL PM

1 2 3 4 5 6 7 8 9 10

STRESS LEVEL PM

1 2 3 4 5 6 7 8 9 10

TODAY I HAD

	little	enough
water	☐	☐
fruits	☐	☐
vegetables	☐	☐
sleep	☐	☐
fresh air	☐	☐
free time	☐	☐
	☐	☐

👍 POSITIVE EXPERIENCES TODAY

○ success at work   ○ sports activity
○ meeting with friends ○ good weather
○ time for family   ○ time in nature
○ excursion   ○ delicious food
○ _____   ○ _____

💬 NEGATIVE EXPERIENCES TODAY

○ failure at work   ○ loneliness
○ dispute   ○ bad weather
○ criticism   ○ bad food
○ exclusion   ○ fears
○ _____   ○ _____

WHAT CAN I DO TO MAKE MY NEXT DAY BETTER?

_____

_____

THOUGHTS & REFLECTIONS

_____

_____

_____

_____

DATE: _____   DAY: M T W T F S S

Daily *Mood* Tracker

TODAY I FEEL

- ☐ grateful
- ☐ happy
- ☐ proud
- ☐ motivated
- ☐ productive
- ☐ relaxed
- ☐ satisfied
- ☐ calm
- ☐ powerful
- ☐ lonely
- ☐ depressed
- ☐ anxious
- ☐ sad
- ☐ angry
- ☐ annoyed
- ☐ tired
- ☐ _____
- ☐ _____

WHY DO I FEEL THIS WAY?

_____

_____

THREE GOALS FOR TODAY

1 _____

2 _____

3 _____

MOOD AM
☺ ☺ ☺ ☹ ☺ ☹ ☹

ENERGY LEVEL AM
1 2 3 4 5 6 7 8 9 10

STRESS LEVEL AM
1 2 3 4 5 6 7 8 9 10

MOOD PM
☺ ☺ ☺ ☹ ☺ ☹ ☹

ENERGY LEVEL PM
1 2 3 4 5 6 7 8 9 10

STRESS LEVEL PM
1 2 3 4 5 6 7 8 9 10

TODAY I HAD

	little	enough
water	☐	☐
fruits	☐	☐
vegetables	☐	☐
sleep	☐	☐
fresh air	☐	☐
free time	☐	☐
	☐	☐

👍 POSITIVE EXPERIENCES TODAY

- ○ success at work
- ○ meeting with friends
- ○ time for family
- ○ excursion
- ○ _____
- ○ sports activity
- ○ good weather
- ○ time in nature
- ○ delicious food
- ○ _____

👎 NEGATIVE EXPERIENCES TODAY

- ○ failure at work
- ○ dispute
- ○ criticism
- ○ exclusion
- ○ _____
- ○ loneliness
- ○ bad weather
- ○ bad food
- ○ fears
- ○ _____

WHAT CAN I DO TO MAKE MY NEXT DAY BETTER?

_____

_____

THOUGHTS & REFLECTIONS

_____

_____

_____

_____

DATE: _____

Daily *Mood* Tracker

DAY: M T W T F S S

TODAY I FEEL

- ☐ grateful
- ☐ happy
- ☐ proud
- ☐ motivated
- ☐ productive
- ☐ relaxed
- ☐ satisfied
- ☐ calm
- ☐ powerful
- ☐ lonely
- ☐ depressed
- ☐ anxious
- ☐ sad
- ☐ angry
- ☐ annoyed
- ☐ tired
- ☐ _____
- ☐ _____

WHY DO I FEEL THIS WAY?

_____

_____

THREE GOALS FOR TODAY

1 _____

2 _____

3 _____

MOOD AM

☺ ☺ ☺ ☹ ☹ ☹ ☹

ENERGY LEVEL AM

1 2 3 4 5 6 7 8 9 10

STRESS LEVEL AM

1 2 3 4 5 6 7 8 9 10

MOOD PM

☺ ☺ ☺ ☹ ☹ ☹ ☹

ENERGY LEVEL PM

1 2 3 4 5 6 7 8 9 10

STRESS LEVEL PM

1 2 3 4 5 6 7 8 9 10

TODAY I HAD

	little	enough
water	☐	☐
fruits	☐	☐
vegetables	☐	☐
sleep	☐	☐
fresh air	☐	☐
free time	☐	☐
	☐	☐

👍 POSITIVE EXPERIENCES TODAY

- ○ success at work
- ○ meeting with friends
- ○ time for family
- ○ excursion
- ○ _____
- ○ sports activity
- ○ good weather
- ○ time in nature
- ○ delicious food
- ○ _____

💬 NEGATIVE EXPERIENCES TODAY

- ○ failure at work
- ○ dispute
- ○ criticism
- ○ exclusion
- ○ _____
- ○ loneliness
- ○ bad weather
- ○ bad food
- ○ fears
- ○ _____

WHAT CAN I DO TO MAKE MY NEXT DAY BETTER?

_____

_____

THOUGHTS & REFLECTIONS

_____

_____

_____

_____

DATE: _____   DAY: M T W T F S S

Daily Mood Tracker

TODAY I FEEL

☐ grateful   ☐ motivated   ☐ satisfied   ☐ lonely   ☐ sad   ☐ tired
☐ happy   ☐ productive   ☐ calm   ☐ depressed   ☐ angry   ☐ _____
☐ proud   ☐ relaxed   ☐ powerful   ☐ anxious   ☐ annoyed   ☐ _____

WHY DO I FEEL THIS WAY?

_____

_____

THREE GOALS FOR TODAY

1 _____

2 _____

3 _____

MOOD AM

😀 🙂 😐 🙁 😵 😟 😣

ENERGY LEVEL AM

1 2 3 4 5 6 7 8 9 10

STRESS LEVEL AM

1 2 3 4 5 6 7 8 9 10

MOOD PM

😀 🙂 😐 🙁 😵 😟 😣

ENERGY LEVEL PM

1 2 3 4 5 6 7 8 9 10

STRESS LEVEL PM

1 2 3 4 5 6 7 8 9 10

TODAY I HAD

	little	enough
water	☐	☐
fruits	☐	☐
vegetables	☐	☐
sleep	☐	☐
fresh air	☐	☐
free time	☐	☐
	☐	☐

👍 POSITIVE EXPERIENCES TODAY

○ success at work   ○ sports activity
○ meeting with friends ○ good weather
○ time for family   ○ time in nature
○ excursion   ○ delicious food
○ _____   ○ _____

👎 NEGATIVE EXPERIENCES TODAY

○ failure at work   ○ loneliness
○ dispute   ○ bad weather
○ criticism   ○ bad food
○ exclusion   ○ fears
○ _____   ○ _____

WHAT CAN I DO TO MAKE MY NEXT DAY BETTER?

_____

_____

THOUGHTS & REFLECTIONS

_____

_____

_____

_____

DATE: _____   DAY: M T W T F S S

Daily *Mood* Tracker

TODAY I FEEL

☐ grateful   ☐ motivated   ☐ satisfied   ☐ lonely   ☐ sad   ☐ tired
☐ happy   ☐ productive   ☐ calm   ☐ depressed   ☐ angry   ☐ _____
☐ proud   ☐ relaxed   ☐ powerful   ☐ anxious   ☐ annoyed   ☐ _____

WHY DO I FEEL THIS WAY?

_____

_____

THREE GOALS FOR TODAY

1 _____

2 _____

3 _____

MOOD AM

😁 🙂 😐 😕 😖 😟 ☹️

ENERGY LEVEL AM

1 2 3 4 5 6 7 8 9 10

STRESS LEVEL AM

1 2 3 4 5 6 7 8 9 10

MOOD PM

😁 🙂 😐 😕 😖 😟 ☹️

ENERGY LEVEL PM

1 2 3 4 5 6 7 8 9 10

STRESS LEVEL PM

1 2 3 4 5 6 7 8 9 10

TODAY I HAD

	little	enough
water	☐	☐
fruits	☐	☐
vegetables	☐	☐
sleep	☐	☐
fresh air	☐	☐
free time	☐	☐
	☐	☐

👍 POSITIVE EXPERIENCES TODAY

○ success at work   ○ sports activity
○ meeting with friends ○ good weather
○ time for family   ○ time in nature
○ excursion   ○ delicious food
○ _____   ○ _____

💬 NEGATIVE EXPERIENCES TODAY

○ failure at work   ○ loneliness
○ dispute   ○ bad weather
○ criticism   ○ bad food
○ exclusion   ○ fears
○ _____   ○ _____

WHAT CAN I DO TO MAKE MY NEXT DAY BETTER?

_____

_____

THOUGHTS & REFLECTIONS

_____

_____

_____

_____

DATE: _____

DAY: M T W T F S S

Daily *Mood* Tracker

TODAY I FEEL

☐ grateful　☐ motivated　☐ satisfied　☐ lonely　☐ sad　☐ tired
☐ happy　☐ productive　☐ calm　☐ depressed　☐ angry　☐ _____
☐ proud　☐ relaxed　☐ powerful　☐ anxious　☐ annoyed　☐ _____

WHY DO I FEEL THIS WAY?

_____

_____

THREE GOALS FOR TODAY

❶ _____

❷ _____

❸ _____

MOOD AM
☺ ☺ ☺ ☺ ☺ ☺ ☹

ENERGY LEVEL AM
1 2 3 4 5 6 7 8 9 10

STRESS LEVEL AM
1 2 3 4 5 6 7 8 9 10

MOOD PM
☺ ☺ ☺ ☺ ☺ ☺ ☹

ENERGY LEVEL PM
1 2 3 4 5 6 7 8 9 10

STRESS LEVEL PM
1 2 3 4 5 6 7 8 9 10

TODAY I HAD

	little	enough
water	☐	☐
fruits	☐	☐
vegetables	☐	☐
sleep	☐	☐
fresh air	☐	☐
free time	☐	☐
	☐	☐

👍 POSITIVE EXPERIENCES TODAY

○ success at work　　○ sports activity
○ meeting with friends　○ good weather
○ time for family　　○ time in nature
○ excursion　　　　○ delicious food
○ _____　○ _____

👎 NEGATIVE EXPERIENCES TODAY

○ failure at work　○ loneliness
○ dispute　　　　○ bad weather
○ criticism　　　○ bad food
○ exclusion　　　○ fears
○ _____　○ _____

WHAT CAN I DO TO MAKE MY NEXT DAY BETTER?

_____

_____

THOUGHTS & REFLECTIONS

_____

_____

_____

_____

Imprint:

Serge Ebert is represented by:
NAME: SERGEJ EIBERT | ADRESS: 2880 W OAKLAND PARK BLVD STE 225C,
OAKLAND PARK, FL 33311
E-mail: s.eibert@outlook.com | Editon: 1st editon

Made in United States
Troutdale, OR
12/07/2023